ADVANCE PRAISE FOR *MY JOURNEY THROUGH WAR AND PEACE*

"At twenty-two, Melissa Burch headed to Afghanistan with a camera... determined to film a war for CBS and to find herself. [This] is the dizzying and dazzling account of that journey."
— *Foreword Reviews*

"An absorbing, well-written memoir by a brave adventurer who discovered her own life."
— *Kirkus Reviews*

"Personal growth, international events, the power of images and of individual experience ... Burch's Journey... [shows] how strange connections can shape the future of both individuals and nations. A great read, highly recommended."
— Davide Mana, *Karavansara Blog*

"Melissa's... account of travels into Afghanistan, Soviet Union, and living as a filmmaker in the NYC 80's art scene is intense, raw and enchanting. She has a story that must be told and she does so with a new and charismatic voice."
— Susana Aikin, Emmy Award winning documentary filmmaker of *Transformations*

"Melissa's true life story is not only fascinating, but she had me riveted to every word on the page. Her openness to exploring new horizons... eliciting meaning out of her experiences, and incorporating the lessons in the next step of her journey are totally relevant to the needs of all of us today."
— Kate Soudant, Editor

"Melissa Burch's memoir is the best memoir I have read since *Girl in the Dark* ... In our materialistic culture, about five hundred books a day are published and most of them have all the depth of a mud puddle. This work is a welcome change. Burch's psychological insights are very astute."
— Ryan Tilley, Poet

"Moments like jewels–the lovemaking, of course, how could I not love that! Other kinds of jewels, too. The memoir shares insights in a direct and down-to-earth way. In between the reflections of a young woman's challenging adventure-cum-career as a filmmaker in a war zone are phenomena, life beyond ourselves, shining forth."

– *Yarrow*, Editor

"It's a frustrating, disillusioning, and yet enlightening journey. [Melissa Burch] has harrowing experiences and unexpected joys and successes. And when she is home again, there's both more enlightenment and more harrowing emotional experiences."

– Lis Carey, *Lis Carey's Library blog*

"A difficult relationship with her father and her mother's plunge into alcoholism led Burch to strike out on her own, running from her struggles and desperately searching for meaning.... Burch takes us along on some of the formative times of her life and leaves us asking for the next chapter."

– Mark P Sadler, author of *Kettle of Vultures*

MY JOURNEY THROUGH WAR AND PEACE

Library and Archives Canada Cataloguing in Publication

Burch, Melissa, 1961-, author
    My journey through war and peace : explorations of a young filmmaker, feminist and spiritual seeker / Melissa Burch.

Issued in print and electronic formats.
ISBN 978-1-77161-177-0 (paperback).--ISBN 978-1-77161-178-7 (html).-- ISBN 978-1-77161-179-4 (pdf)

    1. Burch, Melissa, 1961-. 2. Women journalists--United States--Biography. 3. Women war correspondents--United States--Biography. 4. Afghanistan-- History--Soviet Occupation, 1979-1989--Journalists--Biography. I. Title.

PN4874.B87A3 2016   070.4'333092   C2015-906903-3
                                                 C2015-906904-1

Pubished by Mosaic Press, Oakville, Ontario, Canada, © 2016.
Distributed in the United States by Bookmasters (www.bookmasters.com).
Distributed in the U.K. by Roundhouse Group (https://www.roundhousegroup.co.uk).

MOSAIC PRESS, Publishers
Copyright © 2016 Melissa C. Burch

Printed and Bound in Canada.
Cover design and layout by Shasti O'Leary-Soudant
Interior design by Shasti O'Leary-Soudant and Eric Normann. Interior layout by Eric Normann

We acknowledge the Ontario Media Development Corporation for their support of our publishing program

We acknowledge the Ontario Arts Council for their support of our publishing program

ONTARIO ARTS COUNCIL
CONSEIL DES ARTS DE L'ONTARIO
an Ontario government agency
un organisme du gouvernement de l'Ontario

We acknowledge the financial support of the Government of Canada through the Canada Book Fund (CBF) for this project.

Nous reconnaissons l'aide financière du gouvernement du Canada par l'entremise du Fonds du livre du Canada (FLC) pour ce projet.

 Canadian Patrimoine
Heritage canadien

Canada

MOSAIC PRESS
1252 Speers Road, Units 1 & 2
Oakville, Ontario L6L 5N9
phone: (905) 825-2130

info@mosaic-press.com

www.mosaic-press.com

MY JOURNEY THROUGH WAR AND PEACE

Explorations of a
Young Filmmaker, Feminist,
and Spiritual Seeker

Melissa C. Burch

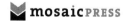 **mosaicPRESS**

For George and Alex, who bring so much love and light into my life

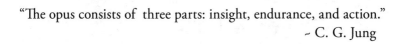

"The opus consists of three parts: insight, endurance, and action."

~ C. G. Jung

CONTENTS

Some details and names have been changed to protect the identities of key players in this memoir or because of imprecise memories.

FIRST PART

INSIGHT BEGUN

"Emotion is the chief source of all becoming-conscious."
~ C. G. Jung

CHAPTER 1

AFGHANISTAN AMBUSH

On the dirt floor, seven bearded 19- to 20-year-old men, my roommates, slept shoulder to shoulder, swaddled in brown wool blankets. Their antiquated Soviet-made Kalashnikov AK-47 automatic rifles rested by their sides, the triggers in safety-lock position. These Afghani freedom fighters had spent the previous night planning a surprise morning attack on a Soviet caravan. Now they rested, saving their strength. A half moon shone through the open window of the one-room mud house. We were in Kandahar, an Afghan region near the Afghan-Pakistan border that was a front line in the war against the Soviet invasion.

Muslim, the Afghani commander in Pakistan, had arranged for the mujahedeen to bring enough weapons for a battle, which I would film. But as each hour brought me closer to the approaching battle, I flipped from lying on my right side to my left side inside my goose down sleeping bag in the back of the room. The mujahedeen seemed as edgy as I was. They were getting up more frequently during the early hours before dawn. I opened my eyes each time a mujahedeen coughed or another went outside to pee or pray. Extra prayers to Allah relieved some of their restlessness. Nothing helped me feel OK in my skin.

As the hour crept towards dawn, I smelled smoke and heard a crackling fire. The men were waking, but even the crackling fire, smell of smoke, and signs of green tea in-the-making could not entice me to leave my warm sleeping bag. Instead, I scooted over a few feet so I could rest my back against the dirt wall and switched on the flashlight. Iridescent dust particles shimmered in the beam of light.

In 1979, under the pretext of wanting to liberate Afghan communists and fight Islamic extremists, the Soviet Union had staged an invasion. In reality, they were after valuable natural resources—natural gas, uranium, iron ore, and copper—and easier access for trade with India and the Middle East. It was now 1982. A week ago, I had turned twenty-one years old on the border dividing Afghanistan and Pakistan. When I learned of the Afghanistan opportunity, I made a promise to myself to be an eyewitness to a war, be a camera person, go beyond my self-doubt as a woman filmmaker who hadn't made a film outside of film school, yet.

In this remote wilderness, I wanted to discover an aspect of myself that felt whole, strong, and confident. And there was something stronger, a magnetic force drawing me to adventure, to a future unknown. It was exhilarating to be present in the moment, to breathe in a zone free of constraints and labels, and to be removed from family obligations to help my teenage sister and younger brother, who were having a tough time with my divorced parents. Afghanistan would be a launching pad into my real adult life.

Leaning against the wall in the hideout house, I gathered myself, took a deep breath and noticed that there was a stretching, pulling, and flipping sensation in my stomach, like a reptile swishing its scaly tail. The sensation bordered on terror, a high-pitched battle cry. In the morning, I would shoot my first war footage for TV. Anchorman Dan Rather from the CBS Evening News had commissioned the story for the U.S. market. Two years earlier, Rather had succeeded in being the first U.S. television journalist to get inside Afghanistan immediately after the Soviet invasion. The televised one-minute news clip showed him standing across the border after he snuck in disguised in Afghani clothes. He was one of the few U.S. journalists who had covered Afghanistan. If everything went well, my footage would be broadcast on CBS for the third-year anniversary of the Soviet invasion. I thought my role as a camerawoman in this war zone was to be the unprejudiced observer, follow the mujahedeen into battle, and show the American public what was really happening. "Inshallah." God willing.

* * *

I had arrived in Kandahar province the previous night with Maria, an old Hungarian friend from film school. She was the rare student who had left the Eastern Bloc and crossed the Iron Curtain all by herself, bootstrapping a scholarship to the London International Film School. With similar resourcefulness, she was now establishing herself as an international war correspondent. Maria's round baby face and henna dyed hair made her look innocent, giving no hint of her self-serving agenda.

The year before, Maria, George—a Greek man I met at film school who would later become my husband—and George's friend John, a fledging British journalist, were planning to make a documentary about Afghanistan's Soviet invasion from the rebel perspective for the BBC. They all got together to explore how to capture this story, a dangerous proposition for any filmmaker or journalist. Since BBC staff producers and veteran film crews didn't usually travel with guerilla groups, this freelance gig would be a way to break into the business. I hadn't gone with George, John, and Maria on the first trip—having just started my first film job for a United Way industrial film producer in my hometown of Washington, D.C. When they returned from Afghanistan, I offered to help. I called up the three major networks—CBS, NBC, and ABC in New York City—and told the producers about their war footage: dead Russians rotting in the hot sun, flies covering their bodies, a shot-down Soviet helicopter, charred and cracked open, and overflowing refugee camps in Pakistan with children covered in dirt and running around in torn clothes. They were gruesome images which did not connect to any reality I had known and did not prepare me for this assignment.

NBC News gave the highest bid for the U.S. rights, an easy sell, even for a girl with no real producing experience. Maria followed up my contact with NBC and pocketed the money. Later, I found out that George and John never saw the royalties from my sale.

When Maria's French cameraman for her next trip was a no-show, she called me in a panic to take his place. I jumped at the chance. I no longer had a job and was living with my father while looking for work. I had left my associate producer job when it became clear that the work was more about paper filing and answering the phone than production opportunities.

Maria was already in London, working on the final arrangements with the BBC. At the CBS headquarters in New York City, I shook hands with Dan Rather after signing the contract at the legal department. I promised him that we would bring back the footage for this planned broadcast on time.

Maria and I had agreed that I would shoot the battle footage and take the photographs. She would be in charge of everything else and would handle the sales and distribution of the war footage to CBS and other worldwide TV networks. Since this would be my first freelance assignment, I would make $3,000 from the photo sales. Maria would keep all the film footage and own the copyrights. She was expecting to make $20,000 or more depending on how many countries' networks bought it.

While this was my first time in Afghanistan, Maria, who was twenty-seven years old, had traveled extensively throughout this 20,000 square mile region of southeast Afghanistan. She had made the first contact with Commander Muslim. Both of them spoke fluent Russian and had a special rapport. Muslim, head of a large Pashtun tribe, had arranged all of the past battle scenes that Maria had filmed. He was in charge of our Afghani companions who came from Kandahar and the nearby villages; they had banded together to battle the Soviets and kick them out of their tribal lands.

The previous night, Maria and I had crossed the Pakistani border with the mujahedeen in a Land Rover. We had driven all day to a fairy tale-like house in a remote Kandahar village where we were spending the night. Our cook, who traveled with us, prepared a basic menu, which would become our daily meal: boiled lamb and, if we were lucky, baked bread. Doc, the Afghani commander who brought us across the border, jokingly promised, "sabaa, sabaa, tomorrow we'll have a real Afghani dinner," after one of our boiled lamb dinners.

During dinner, Maria was quiet. Her eyes darted from the blazing fire in front of us to me, sticking stale bread into a bowl of boiled lamb. She did not eat. When the fire cracked like a gunshot, Maria jumped. Her face froze. She was a closed type and didn't share emotions, strategies, or her personal agendas openly with me.

After dinner, Maria and I walked over behind the large boulders that marked the end of the road. Maria's usual I-know-more-than-you attitude had turned from unshakable confidence to triggered panic. When faced with the reality of being in the middle of a battle for a third time, she didn't think her luck would hold out. My mind wavered between thinking, "How the hell did I get here?" and "What the hell should I do now?"

I had trusted Maria and knew her experience would make the mission easier. Our plan was to film an ambush and, if possible, a shot-down helicopter. Doc knew that, for his group to be taken seriously, he had to follow the military orders of Commander Muslim, the Afghani leader who stayed behind safely in Pakistan and orchestrated our trip inside Afghanistan. The commands were clear: Make sure Melissa gets footage of an ambush that will help the Afghan Freedom Fighter cause. And Maria knew how to make the big dollars—by extending as many minutes as possible of combat footage for a bigger sale to the networks.

But now Maria was saying, "I can't do it this time. You'll have to do this alone." She would not look me in the eye. Her gruff statement ripped into my frail confidence, but I would not show it. I didn't want to look weak in front of her or the mujahedeen. I thought I needed to be warrior-like to succeed.

Maria pulled out a pack of cigarettes. She offered me one, even though she knew I didn't smoke. She turned to face the boulders to light her cigarette. The lighter would not catch. Her usual competency and bravado were shattered. She pocketed the cigarette. Then, she explained how she was too nervous to risk her life again. She couldn't be part of a small group of poorly armed Afghans, as they went up against a modern army. And she had a point. Some of the mujahedeen carried 1940s British rifles that they planned to use against Soviet tanks.

"You'll be fine," were her parting words to me, as she mounted a military- green motorbike to join a mujahedeen driver. Her words didn't make sense, though. Red dust flew behind them, as she fled Afghanistan as fast as she could. I didn't protest. I was in shock and stuck in tough girl mode. I would be fine, I reassured myself. My purpose was clear: to get my story, an honest account of what was happening in Afghanistan.

But my confidence kept vacillating, "How the hell did I get here?" As the sound of the driver's motorbike quickly faded in the distance, a mujahedeen shouted at me to come look behind the boulders. I grabbed my Bolex camera, wound it up, and shot the cook as he sliced the neck of a black goat, making one deliberate cut. The small beast was lying on the ground, its scraggly limbs tied to a leafless tree with a twine rope. The cut stopped its anxious baying, and a gurgled cry came as the crimson blood poured out of its matted neck.

I didn't want to show the men that I was afraid of watching a killing. Instead, I filmed a small mammal slaughtered in front of me. Up until that moment, I had thought of war as what you see on TV, not actual killing and death. The reality of what I was going to see started to sink in.

* * *

As I anticipated the next morning's battle, I thought of my mother. She had pleaded for me not to board the 747 plane in London for Pakistan. She had sounded sober on the long distance, echoey phone call, not slurring her words as she did in her usual alcoholic state.

Our usual mother/daughter communications were mostly one-sided—complaining letters she typed on the same manual typewriter she had used for term papers while a student at Smith College. The M and N bulged like buck teeth above the other letters, chastising me for using the American Express card she loaned me for emergencies only. She hand-signed these letters "Mother," in royal blue ink. I felt I didn't need her permission for anything, not since I had left home when she and my father divorced four years previously. She could not tell me what to do anymore.

My father, on the other hand, had no problem with me going off to a war zone. He was second generation military and had graduated in the first class of the Air Force Academy. In 1962, when I was less than a year old, my father was stationed at the Air Force base in Oakland, CA, where he was a navigator on fighter planes. My grandfather had been captain of a Naval ship in Nagasaki, after the atomic bomb disaster, and an officer at Pearl Harbor before that. In my grandfather's photo album were gory pictures of Japanese soldiers killed in the streets and party scenes of American soldiers dressed up for luaus in the South Pacific. He had juxtaposed the horrific scenes on one side of the black pages with celebratory scenes on the other side. When I opened the album, I saw peace mounted on the left and war on the right.

Lying awake in my sleeping bag, my stomach rumbling from poor digestion of the fatty lamb, my mind shifted to calmer times when my father cooked elaborate French cuisine dinners. After dinner, my mother often worked late on intricate financial projection reports for the Federal Reserve Board, where she had been appointed the first female economist. My father read fairy tales from the *Red Fairy Book*, while I leaned close to him in my bed before falling asleep.

My favorite fairy tale was "Snowdrop," the Andrew Lang early version of "Snow White." Snowdrop's caring mother pricks her finger and, upon seeing red blood, makes a wish that the child she is carrying will have skin as white as the snow, cheeks as red as the blood, and hair and eyes as black as the ebony window frame. Not long after her daughter is born, the mother dies.

* * *

My thoughts drifted back to Maria's sudden departure. She had left me alone here. I automatically got up and went to find the men for some company and to shake off the feeling of abandonment. A warm cup of tea would help, too.

On this dry, crisp morning, my place in this new world with these men was still uncertain. It had almost the quality of a fairy tale about it. The dirt house where we were staying, the black kettle hanging over an open fire, and one woman living among a band of men seemed like a scene from the Disney version of *Snow White and the Seven Dwarfs*. But I was no Sleeping Beauty, with my unwashed brown hair and overweight body, and the tall and robust mujahedeen were hardly the seven dwarves. Frankly, I couldn't remember any of their real names so I gave these brave men childish nicknames.

There was Sleepy, whose black eyes blinked a lot. He cooked our first meal, the night Maria left. He was tending the fire and did most of the cooking during our trip. Steam rose out of the snout of the black kettle, and he poured hot green tea from the kettle into a glass for me. As I sipped my tea, tight-lipped Grumpy stared at me as if I had trespassed in his forest. Doc, the Commander, was a bulky handsome guy who spoke some English and was highly respected by his men. His trimmed black beard and mustache covered his face like a black velvet hem around his cheeks and chin. He was busy handing out the ammunition for his men to carry in the bandoliers across their shoulders. Dopey had blackened teeth, coughed loudly, and stayed up half the night smoking opium. Happy, a gangly teenager, was my favorite, a fearless driver who smiled a lot. Two nights before, he had navigated over rough terrain with no headlights— avoiding villages and their barking dogs, fording dry riverbeds by moonlight—to deliver Maria and me to Doc and his men.

There was no Bashful or Sneezy, just two crazy guys who were not allowed to fight because they had lost their minds. One had shot and killed his wife. The other bragged about how he had killed Russians by twisting the handle of a black umbrella that popped its spider web canvas open. (Had he seen this in a James Bond movie?) Being from the same Pashtun tribe, these two men were full-fledged members of our group, never to be left behind. They were jihadists, and like the other mujahedeen, they were guaranteed a place in heaven if they were killed in this holy war. They were just not allowed to carry any dangerous weapons. I didn't believe in heaven, only an existential hope that there was more to life than war and peace.

In this war zone, my gut-wrenching anxiety was like a tsunami that I steered towards, turning it into a great wave that I wanted to ride to safety. Adventure was a way to numb the anxiety. I pushed for greater thrills to relieve a gaping hole in my solar plexus. I'd been anxious ever since age eleven, when a fire had destroyed my family's kitchen, put my father in the hospital, and changed all our lives into Before and After. The volume was not normally turned up so loud; usually, it was more like the rumbling of a 747 jet.

Now I'd ridden the anxiety to Afghanistan. Each adventure that called me was an opportunity to test myself, validate my existence, and connect to something much greater than myself. I experienced this as a kind of an obligation, a giant positiveness filling my body, my cells pulsating, freedom beckoning, as I said "YES" to each new idea.

But that didn't mean I was without worry. The angst was there always, even while the "YES" brought clarity and opportunities. I'd settled on a kind of counter-intuitive balance, a letting go, my own version of non-attachment: Use fear to release fear, discover a new self, and reach a state of wonder.

* * *

Outside the rustic house, the soldiers and I stood looking at the first rays of the morning sun in the sky, a splash of orange-yellow light. Large reddish boulders blocked the dirt road. There was no turning back. The anxiety that kept me up in the night had to be suppressed. I had to go forward, take up my camera, and shoot.

The sun was rising and the sunbeams blinded my eyes. I grabbed my sunglasses out of my backpack. My Ray-Ban knockoffs, bought in New York City's Chinatown, instantly made me stand out. Otherwise, the mujahedeen and I dressed alike, in earth tone pajama suits with ropes tied around our waists to keep our baggy pants up. The major difference was that I wore a long tunic tightly stretched over my size 40DDD bra. Patu wool blankets hung over our shoulders like wrapped prayer shawls. Our uniforms included deflated, soufflé-shaped wool caps. You could buy these Afghani hats at any flea market in the U.S. Instead of a Soviet automatic rifle, I transported an old-fashioned 16mm wind-up Bolex film camera.

My first day of battle. The whole trip until now had been preparation for this upcoming ambush on a Soviet convoy. I was not filming refugee camps or interviewing commanders in Pakistan or standing on the border for a photo op like Dan Rather. I was partaking in a guerrilla ambush, late in the season, when the mujahedeen had usually stopped fighting.

Standing, drinking my glass of tea, now cold and bitter, I watched the mujahedeen lay out their patu blankets on the ground, in single file. They faced Mecca, knelt, and prostrated. Doc led the group invocation. I stood alone. The only woman. The only foreigner.

I didn't believe in a paternalistic God to beseech to spare our lives. My God was all around us. A force in nature. What was meant to happen would happen. Death was beyond our control. I didn't believe prayers could change the outcome or that a martyr's death pleased God more than any other death.

Fumbling in my blue backpack, I grabbed the roll of stiff Pakistani toilet paper, left the men praying, and hurried to the bathroom. The wooden outhouse had a hole on a board. The manure gasses permeated the tiny room. The stench was unbearable but a strong breeze pushed the putrid smell through the slats in the wooden wall.

When I returned, Sleepy poured each of us a fresh helping of hot green tea in short French tumbler glasses filled halfway with refined white sugar. No stirring allowed. Before the next refill, a luxurious syrup sweetened the last sips. A piece of day-old Afghani flatbread completed the breakfast. It was almost time to leave.

I double checked that the Bolex 16mm film camera was loaded, cranked tight, and ready to roll. Then, I went through my inventory. The Canon 35mm still camera, 20 rolls of 16mm film, 10 rolls of 35mm film, and a black bag for changing the movie film were safely packed in the backpack. The film equipment and stock had been donated by CBS. The still rolls came from Time magazine. The 35mm camera was mine. My familiar tools of the trade were prepped.

Commander Doc, honorable as an ambassador, held authority over all of us in a tough-love mode; calm and strict, he handed out the prime weapon. He opened a dented, large, green metal box and passed the fifteen-pound RPG-7 rocket launcher to Grumpy. Doc's plan, an attack on a nearby convoy, hinged on Grumpy. Grumpy slung the weapon over his shoulder effortlessly, as if he were bounding into his backyard woods to shoot a squirrel with his brand new slingshot. He would have to fire a warhead that would destroy a Soviet armed vehicle, preferably a tank—a military prize for the mujahedeen.

Doc calculated each attack on the basis of its purpose and his anemic military supplies. He weighed the benefits and losses of the surefire retaliation the Soviets would wreak on local villages. In this case, Doc needed me to capture the Soviet tank attack on film—otherwise known as "blood and guts" footage—to appeal to Western news agencies. The agencies would publicize the Afghan cause, and the hope was that the United States, and possibly Pakistan and China, would send much needed military arms, in response.

The mujahedeen had their supplies ready: over 1000 rounds of AK-47 steel-cased ammunition. Each fighter carried about eight pounds of bullets across his chest. Doc had formed this group three years ago, immediately after the Soviet invasion, when Commander Muslim, the local tribal leader, called him to lead. Doc picked strong men who understood guerrilla warfare. The motto was: "Sting your opponent, get some attention, and then clear out."

Our motley gang in our pajama-style pants and tunics surrounded Doc. The mujahedeen hoisted their rifles and their Kalashnikovs across their shoulders, ready for the signal to move out. We looked more like Robin Hood's bandits than a military operation ready to attack the Soviet Union, the Evil Empire that now occupied Afghanistan. Doc posed for me while I took still photos of him standing erect with his gun. He looked strong and fierce, in spite of his casual outfit. His dark brown eyes met mine and held my gaze steadily. He was experienced, having led this kind of action numerous times. I lacked experience but, as I faced him with my camera, there was mutual respect.

A skinny nine-year-old boy, with darting, star-like eyes, ran panting into the middle of our camp shouting in Pashtu, the local language, "The Russians are coming." In response, the men yelled the chorus, "Allahu Akbar." God is greatest.

Doc led the way down a dirt path lined with pomegranate trees and mud-baked houses on either side. He was followed by Grumpy, carrying the oversized prized weapon, then me with the cameras. Dopey, Sleepy, and the rest of the mujahedeen, including the two crazy guys, brought up the rear. We walked purposefully, swaggering out in the open under the winter sun. Staring at the bright ball, I tried to absorb the sun's energy. Then, as I briefly shut my eyes, black spots appeared on the horizon.

As we marched by a village, a gaggle of dirty children in colorful rags stood upright and stiff like small soldiers. The neighborhood was a cross between ancient-looking mud buildings and a modern trailer park, so run-down that there was no landscaping—no grass, no plants. The village was covered in a layer of beige dust, a monochrome site. In the distance, a mother screamed for her brood. The children ran in a pack in the direction of her voice. At the side of the road, an old man with a white beard bent over his work, repairing shoes. He focused intently, hitting tiny brass nails into the heel of a worn-out shoe. He didn't look up, even as I, a Western woman carrying a camera and surrounded by Afghani guerrilla fighters—not exactly a common sight—walked by.

After a few blocks, we stopped in front of a row of three abandoned dirt buildings, flat topped and shaped like giant, rectangular Lego pieces. Afghani villagers once stored cloths, canned foods, piles of grains, and orange, yellow, and red spices in burlap sacks in these storehouses. Now, these simple structures were empty shells abandoned for demolition. The villagers knew they were too exposed to potential attacks to be used anymore.

The Soviet strategy was to take a few minor hits from the mujahedeen and then destroy village markets, storehouses, and homes. Collateral civilian damage. These actions were intended to encourage the people to turn against the mujahedeen and stop hiding them, but the opposite happened. This strategy incited more solidarity among the Afghani people.

The buildings' ghostly front walls stood facing the north side of the Kandahar-Herat highway, one of the few paved roads running through Afghanistan. An occasional car sped by on the two lanes. Doc stood next to a lone, bare tree and motioned for us to move into the storehouses. I took deeper breaths and held them longer, while my heart quickened. I recognized my fear, it was part of me but not in control of me. I moved quickly into place, assessing which building had the best view of the road. Then, I chose the middle mud structure, which had two open windows facing the road where the Soviet trucks, soldiers, and perhaps tanks would drive by, a hundred feet away. I crouched inside the sandy-colored shelter, comprised of dirt floors, four walls, and a roof. My fully loaded camera, tightly wound, was ready to go. I gave it one last crank to make sure.

Grumpy hung outside the buildings, patiently pointing his missile launcher over the roof for an arc-like trajectory. Rumbling started like a small earthquake. I heard loud whispers in Pashtu but couldn't make out any of the words. Dopey ran away, back to the edge of the town, like a deserter; a panic attack had gotten the best of him. The two crazy guys stood by the lone tree, arms folded, waiting for the action to begin.

I pointed my long telephoto lens through an open window at a rainbow steam mirage rising from the pavement. I stared through my camera's viewfinder. I'd been trained to aim and shoot one thing at a time, but never in a war zone. I would need to remember to hold the image steady, in order to succeed in the midst of the chaos that was about to ensue.

The first Soviet military truck passed in front of the storehouse where I was hiding. The open window gave me a perfect view for filming the attack on the convoy. The ruddy, clean-shaven face of the blonde Russian driver looked straight ahead. He was no older than the Afghani mujahedeen. On the passing truck, the red flag stamped with a hammer and sickle and a golden star stood erect, flapping in the wind. Six more trucks followed. No tanks.

Some soldiers rode an open-air, flatbed truck. Ricochet gunfire blasted from both directions. The Soviet soldiers pointed their sleek automatic rifles toward us. The soldier passing in front of my camera had his eyes focused through the rangefinder of his AK-47. It was the first time I saw a loaded gun pointed at me, but I was not afraid. I was breathing deeply and my heart was beating slower. The action slowed time down. My right thumb held the camera button down. The smooth whir, a gentle mechanical sound, assured me that the film inside the metal camera box was capturing the ambush.

I was calm, fearless. I was in a zone that hardened me—I felt invincible and calculating, filled with courage. There was a pause in the matrix, sounds muffled. I had entered an alternate reality, like a ninja who could grab a speeding bullet because it moved in frozen time. I photographed the scene.

A distinctive whirring sound ripped from behind me. Grumpy's warhead had been launched from outside the building. Then there was a loud explosion. He'd done it. Through the window, I saw in my viewfinder that he had hit one of the smaller Soviet trucks. Smoke billowed from the blazing truck. Flint particles flew into the room through the window and scratched my arms. Two Russian soldiers jumped out of the front seat of the truck and dashed away from us. The burning truck blocked the caravan's passage.

After four minutes of shooting, winding the camera crank counter-clockwise every 28 seconds, I heard a loud click. The film flapped on the bottom camera spindle, hitting the inside of the metal box. I grabbed my backpack from the floor and ran outside to sit under the lonely tree in the back of the building. Under a patu blanket, my hands slipped into the sleeves of the black changing bag. I knew what I needed to feel: the smooth canister of 100-foot 16mm film. I unlocked the camera, unhooked the bottom reel, opened the cool metallic can, took out the new roll of film, placed the exposed film in the can, and taped it shut to keep the light out. After threading the fresh film, I measured the loop for the perfect tension using my left thumb and closed up the camera. Just then, a deafening explosion pounded the ground.

The building I had been filming in minutes before was shattered in seconds. Clouds of beige dust covered us, bits of clay flew through the air, and the wooden door fell flat on the ground. The scene was as dreamlike as a Schwarzenegger action film in a Cineplex: mujahedeen soldiers ran through the blast, out of the buildings, leaping from harm. Walls collapsed, the ceiling fell and broke into large pieces, becoming a pile of rubble. Smoky dust was everywhere. But despite the destruction around me, I felt calm. I seemed to have no relation to my healthy body sitting on the ground, felt no connection to the decimated building 40 feet away. Instead, I was pulled into a sense of timelessness, weightlessness, absoluteness.

Nobody on our side had been hurt. Our gang bolted. We grabbed our things and ran, past the shoe repairman, who was still sitting by the side of the road as if it were an ordinary work day. The Soviets did not pursue us. No, that was not how guerrilla warfare worked. They would pick some local village and destroy their livelihood, damage aqueducts, and turn homes into rubble. It was the women, children, and old people who suffered the most in war.

CHAPTER 2

AMONG THE RUINS

After the attack on the Soviet caravan, we split up into twos and threes to avoid detection and lie low for several days. Doc, Dopey, and I waited in hiding for night to fall, then we crept out stealthily, pressing ourselves against the tall village walls. Walking in the middle of the narrow, winding road was like plunging into an abyss of danger—at any moment, we could be recognized by an informer, who would have us arrested. We slipped through an open doorway and into a makeshift shelter for the night. A plump man wearing a grey turban whispered for us to enter. His eyes were blood-shot, and his face looked too young for his grey beard.

In the kerosene light, dust covered the floor where we sat. The rugs were gone. Nothing remained but bare walls with blackened scars. There was no hot food. We ate some stale bread from break-fast. Our host's hand shook as he poured tea into four glasses. It had none of the customary sugar at the bottom. Doc took wrapped hard candy out of his pocket and gave one to each of us to suck on while we drank. Our host refused the offering. He stared at the blank walls. These walls, our Afghani host told us, were all that was still standing after a bombing killed his wife and son. Doc translated for me so I could understand what had happened to this grieving man.

There was no moon shining that night. I fell asleep quickly, instinctively, exhausted from the battle and relieved to be getting some rest at last, lying next to the mujahedeen. I felt safe and protected with Doc nearby.

When we woke up, daylight showed us what had happened to this house. Gaping holes revealed what were once simple living rooms. Wooden beams hung sideways from the roof to the ground, like seatbelts lying across large wooden doors balanced on fallen walls. Helicopters flying overhead were common enough occurrences, but two weeks previously, the Soviets had dropped bombs on this village, in retaliation for the Afghan freedom fighters' hit-and-run strategy. There had been no time to run. Roofs smashed down on unsuspecting and innocent people, killing whole families. Ghosts lived here. And they were not speaking.

* * *

When I was eleven years old, our family kitchen had similar black soot marks as those I saw on the walls of the bombed home.

"Fire!" I shouted.

I ran out of my sister's bedroom and saw flames and black smoke pouring out of the kitchen into the hallway, dining room, and living room. Elena, my eight-year-old sister, followed me. Desperate for help, I ran down our apartment hall, opened the heavy front door, and continued down the long building corridor to the front desk, where Stanley, our Nigerian operator, usually plugged wires into an old-fashioned switchboard so that neighbors could talk to each other on the internal phone lines for free.

But Stanley wasn't there. A new African guy, whom I didn't know, stared at me wide-eyed as though I was a midget in a circus. My voice was high pitched and breathless, "Call 911, there's an emergency."

As I stood there, I tried to make sense of what had happened. Moments before the explosion, my father had been gluing down terracotta tiles on the kitchen floor opposite my sister's room. He was not a DIY type, but once he had an idea for a project, he became an expert. My sister and I were used to expecting the unexpected from our father.

A horizontal funnel-shaped wind, starch-smelling, tunneled through the hallway into my sister's bedroom. An unnatural gust of air blew by where we sat. A cannon bang sounded seconds later, like thunder after lightning. My sister's thick plate-glass window shattered, and a gaping hole opened to the cold March wind. The newfangled glue my father was using to install the tiles had combusted with the stove's gas exhaust. The fire came seconds after the blast. My father was trapped in the burning kitchen and suffered second and third degree burns over forty percent of his body. The shattered four-by-six window formed a gaping hole in our lives, never to be fully patched.

My parents had moved us to The Ontario apartments in D.C.'s Adams Morgan neighborhood in early 1968. My mother had always desired a cosmopolitan city life. She had fallen in love with London when she had lived there as a student, while attending the London School of Economics. Upon returning to the U.S., she was keen to avoid the isolation of the suburbs and the dullness of strip malls. Like her, my father loved all the advantages of big city life. He enjoyed shopping at gourmet stores in Georgetown. He bought first edition French cookbooks (one in particular had a Christmas menu where the zoo animals were cooked during the 1870 Siege of Paris). He would often recreate the recipes for us and leave behind a terrible mess for my sister and me to clean up. My mother, frustrated with the chaos she found when she came home from work, would insist that my sister and I wash the pots stacked on the counters and kitchen floor.

My mother had one of the highest paying government salaries, a federal GS-13 ranked position, but despite her income, our electricity and phone would be cut off for days at a time. My father's expensive tastes, and the highs and lows of his entrepreneurial computer software business, were a constant source of tension in the house.

After the kitchen fire and explosion, my mother, exhausted from working all day, would come home with take-out from the neighborhood Chinese restaurant. My father was incapacitated in the hospital. Our charred kitchen wouldn't be fixed for months. She would spread out my father's paperwork on the mahogany dining table and work late into the night trying to save his struggling business, while sipping on a glass of vodka.

My mother was the breadwinner, a reversal of roles at a time when that was unusual. Locked away in a hospital, my father was no help. His cheery promise of making millions of dollars when his company sold must have felt pretty empty. My mother locked herself in her own resilient world. Always a loner and introvert, she didn't know how to ask for help.

I helped as much as I could. On school mornings, I poured Coco Puffs and milk in bowls for my sister, brother, and me. I packed our school lunches. On Saturdays, I bought bologna, individually-wrapped American cheese, Wonder Bread, Snack Pack chocolate pudding, and carrots. On the floor of the living room, I assembled fifteen sandwiches, inserted each one in a plastic baggie, cut carrots into sticks, bagged them, and put the pudding and everything else in brown paper bags. Then, I stacked all these paper bags in the fridge for daily retrieval before school.

What did my mother do with her fears, worries, panic? She must have found solace in drinking alone—the kids in bed, no one to talk to, sucking it up for tomorrow. The alcohol numbed the pain. There were no real consequences, yet, just a bit of respite in hard times.

Is this when I felt all alone in the world for the first time? When the low-grade rumblings of "not good enough" started? I couldn't fix what had happened. There was no way to restore order. I couldn't bring my father home. I didn't even have the courage to visit him in the hospital. My mother was too busy and focused on the business at hand to nurture or console me or my siblings.

The gaping hole from the fire was a wound that unsettled our family for good. Home had already been a battleground because of my parents' fighting. Of course, the kitchen could be repaired, but there was no quick fix for my mother, who started to lock herself in her bedroom and began drinking earlier and earlier in the evening. A gnawing sensation took hold in my belly, and I started to use food to calm the beast. This solution turned me into a fatso, with more self-defeating anxiety.

My father survived the fire, but my mother never recovered. During my teenage years, she became the crazy witch mother, unpredictable, snarly, volatile, and impossible to please. But, at 11 years old, I was unaware of what was to come.

* * *

After the Afghan ambush on the Soviet caravan, we adopted a nightly ritual of moving from one safe house to another. This was part of Commander Doc's strategy for not endangering any one Afghani household—and to keep us safe.

Doc told me there was a rumor that the Soviets knew there was a female Western journalist in the area. Villagers claimed they heard my name on the radio. Doc told me the broadcasters had used my first name. The Afghan government newscaster, a Soviet propaganda tool, denounced "Melissa" as an American spy. Did they know my last name? The only reliable news was from the BBC broadcasts, which were able to keep straight that the mujahedeen, with their many tribal factions, were unanimously against the Soviet-backed Afghan government.

No, I was not a spy, I was a journalist. But what a strange thought! What would life be like if I were a spy? My 21-year-old self pictured scenarios of being caught by the Soviets and declared dangerous on a Moscow news broadcast. They could throw me in jail, torture me, or just have me disappear without anyone knowing what really happened. I told myself that none of those outcomes had happened. They were not real.

On the fourth day in Kandahar, Dopey, pointy-chinned and twitchy, drove the white Jeep across an arid plateau with spiky hills in the distance to a village twenty miles away. I rode shotgun next to him. Previously captured and tortured in Kabul, Dopey was not the stoic, manly-man commander type made famous by the Afghan defeat of the British in 1842. Soviet Intelligence had shot scarring electric shocks through his body. He was a broken man addicted to opium. Some nights his racking cough woke me.

It was dusk as we drove, and the light cast long shadows on the ochre dirt. The cold wind and falling sun fought each other. Dopey and I were two people alone together, not a conspicuous gang roaming from place to place.

Shaking, Dopey pointed far away at a floating white dot that resembled a UFO. He slammed on the brakes. With the engine turned off, all was quiet. We heard a distant chopping sound approaching us. Dopey's face stretched like a red balloon, eyes dilated, and he inhaled short gasps in staccato intervals, stuttering "Heleeckopter!"—his one word of English—over and over again. Dopey yanked on his door handle and hit the door hard, then again. He was going to kill the door. I wanted to run and hide under my blanket, far from the exposed truck, which I knew was an easy target for the helicopter's bombs. Safety could be as easy as crouching down on the ground and making myself as small a ball as possible under my dirt-colored blanket. Or maybe not. Maybe I should have followed Maria out and not put myself in this kind of danger.

I leaned over Dopey, whose jerking body was convulsing like someone having an epileptic seizure. I pushed the driver's side door wide open. He jumped out of the trap, ran zigzag until he fell on the ground, and threw his patu over himself. I also ran far from the Jeep and threw myself under the brown blanket that I carried everywhere. The whirling tic toc tic toc of the helicopter blades echoed louder and louder. The helicopter, sounding more menacing than any mythical dragon, hovered right above us. But then the sky darkened, as the sun passed behind a large cloud. The pilot didn't want to fly below the clouds. No gunfire or bombs dropped this evening. The helicopter made a U-turn and followed the same route back from where it came.

When Dopey and I were back in the jeep, I felt like I was gliding, as I did when I ice skated as a kid, spinning, raising my arms entwined above my head, adrenaline pumping, leaping and soaring through the air. This war action drug medicated all previous anxiety. I was in the moment, experiencing what was. I was twirling full speed, leaning back into the wind, joyful, giddy, alive.

* * *

I'd been inside Afghanistan for a week, but I had yet to shoot all my footage. Doc kept telling me, "Sabaa, sabaa" (tomorrow, tomorrow). We had planned to film the Mi-24 helicopter shot down near the Soviet post, not far from where Dopey and I had been. "We light helicopter with gasoline, look like just shot by mujahedeen," Doc explained. A shot-down helicopter was a big deal because it was next to impossible to shoot one down with the scant Afghan arms. I was being used to make a sexier war for the mujahedeen. My ethics were stretched thin by this idea of fabricated news, but with a few close-up shots of Grumpy and the RPG 7 missile launcher, the staged scene could look real. Later, I learned that staging for TV news was not that uncommon in war settings.

As a filmmaker, I understood how editing and camera angles could distort time. After I bought my first Super 8 camera in high school, I shot roll after roll to develop my eye. What you chose to leave out was as important as what you left in. The convoy attack would look much more dramatic by editing in training footage, soldiers in battle and explosions. A burning helicopter would be far more captivating than a combusted relic—and more likely to end up on the broadcast than on the cutting room floor. Context and dramatic footage were everything. And in television news, you had 2 to 3 minutes to tell a story, if you were lucky.

Here in Afghanistan, I was on the other side of the news story, the maker not the viewer. I was too young and emotional to be a neutral journalist. I picked sides, and the Soviets were the Evil Empire. They were killing my friends. I had banded together with the mujahedeen like Snow White and her dwarves. I shot the war in Afghanistan. The mujahedeen took care of me in their wild land, while they did their work of attacking the Soviets.

* * *

When I was 16 years old, I took a high school film class and, for one of my assignments, I shot my neighborhood, the inner city. I had bought a Canon 1014XL-S Super 8 camera, top of the line, with my babysitting money. The camera gave me a reason to go into dangerous places. I went alone; none of my friends wanted to join me. Their parents would not have allowed it, anyway, if they knew where I was shooting.

In the late sixties and seventies, D.C. was known as the murder capital of the nation. Enclosed by grey stone walls, our apartment building separated us from the ghetto. Built in 1906, the eclectic Beaux Arts building had two pristine white porches with ionic columns that flanked each side of the garden, manicured green lawns, large evergreen trees, and pink roses that climbed a wooden trellis.

Outside The Ontario apartments' gates, paint peeled off the late 19th century townhouses that had become slum rentals. One front yard featured an enormous pig and speckled chickens, breaking all local ordinances. After the milkman was held up at gunpoint in his little truck with clanking glass bottles in the back, he no longer delivered milk to The Ontario.

On 16th Street, on a hill about fifteen blocks from The Ontario, was the once stately Meridian Hill Park. Here, Joan of Arc rode on horseback from a granite perch, her bronze sword stolen years ago. The graffitied, cascading, terraced fountain, now empty, was nearly regal. The park was drug infested: addicts swooned on benches, needles littered the winter grass, empty syringes were left on the broken walkways. Teetering alcoholics hissed, as I passed. Dante's statue, wearing a cloak, presided over D.C.'s hell. I wanted close-ups of the fallen so I pointed the camera at a taut black face, with features more like a skeleton than a young man's, high on heroin. I zoomed in, and when he came in my direction, I ran the opposite way.

This scary place, these dangerous people, excited me. They were the source for my 10th grade student film at National Cathedral School's all-girls school. I was proud of my work and won an award for memorializing a park at a time in history when Angela Davis tried to rename it Malcolm X Park.

"I want to use film to change the world," I wrote in my red, leather-bound journal after shooting the seedy park film. I saw being a filmmaker as an adventure and felt that documentaries could show the world what needed to be fixed. The camera gave me an excuse and permission to enter foreign worlds, new and exciting places to explore.

* * *

I was frustrated by hearing yet another "sabaa" this morning—tomorrow we'll go to the shot-down helicopter, Doc told me, again. It had been ten days since the ambush, and I was waiting around for nothing. I stormed out of the broken shelter and took my first solo walk since my adoption into the Afghani warrior tribe.

Liberated, I photographed the ghost town. Flocks of birds flew overhead in V formations. Some doorways were left standing, inviting guests into their ruinous compounds, but entering would be too dangerous; the yards were sprinkled with anti-personnel mines. Nothing of value had been left behind, not even a rag, just colorless rubble.

A figure appeared around a corner, walking towards me. I slowly squatted down, leaning against the broken wall, and covered myself with the patu blanket. The other person crouched on the bare ground, exposed. We were sixty feet apart, both frozen on the spot like targets.

The other person turned out to be a woman in her early twenties with the greenest eyes, eyes like those of the National Geographic Afghan girl photographed by Steve McCurry. She peeked out from behind delicate hands. She was not wearing her chador, the large, tent-like sheet with no hand openings, and only a prison grid to see through. Instead, she had on a simple pale yellow embroidered tunic over tight pants.

We were two women meeting on the same road, both afraid that we were going to be found out. Under some fundamentalist tribal laws, she could be stoned for leaving her house without wearing the veil. I could be arrested as a spy. We were so unlike each other—from different cultures and with our own purposes—but we were both young and female and struggling to survive in the moment.

* * *

Exactly seven days after promising to take me to the shot-down helicopter, Sleepy, our cook, came by my shelter leading a huge horse with a blanket and a small rope in its mouth. Now, I would have to find some excuse why they shouldn't set fire to the Mi-24. I had made up my mind that I didn't want to fake anything for CBS News. I thought this, as I struggled to climb on the horse's back with all my camera gear. Doc led the animal into a ditch. I jumped on and then unceremoniously slid off. There was lots of commotion and shouting. Sleepy pulled me out of the ditch. This time, Grumpy, the tough and reliable fighter, shoved my big butt back on the horse. He grabbed a stick to prod the horse, which needed constant coaxing to keep moving. Sleepy rode a bicycle out in front. They were now my official bodyguards. We left Doc and the rest of his gang behind.

We started on this journey around 9 a.m., roaming the barren landscape of rocks and low hills. Then, we trudged next to a creek, its constant bubbling and the horse's rhythmic steps were the only sounds for hours.

"We must get there by 4 o'clock," I told them, looking at my Timex watch, "so there is light for shooting."

"No problem," they said.

On dirt roads parallel to a canal, where bare trees were rooted on the side of the Arghandab River valley outside of Kandahar, we meandered for eight hours. The up and down motion of the horse was constant. My back and butt were achy. I was thirsty, and there was no water.

It was quiet, very few people. Occasionally, a bearded old man with a donkey passed us. The older men stayed behind in the villages with the women and children, while the younger men left their homes and took up arms with a minimum of training and equipment to sting the Super Power like hornets.

The sun was going down. How close were we to the destroyed helicopter? I had no idea, and my companions were not saying. Western notions of time and distance were meaningless to Afghans. We could communicate by hand gestures, and by now I had learned a few simple Pashto words like jhar sa (hurry up), khwahish mikonam (thank you), darawem (stop), and xoral (eat) from the guidebook I brought. However, no real conversation could take place. In the beginning, I relied on Doc for any morsel of information, no matter how sparse. Later, I understood the rhythms of the day and could figure out the most essential communications without falling back on a common language.

I also relied on my guidebook for getting tips on certain local customs. For example, I avoided touching my food with my left hand; it was considered dirty because of its use during toiletry.

I also read about Afghans' struggles and bravery over the centuries. Considered a gateway to the Mediterranean, India, and China along the Silk Road, Afghanistan was envied for its strategic location but was known to be nearly impossible to conquer for long. Legend had it that even Alexander the Great faced strong resistance from the Afghan tribe in 330 BC—"easy to march into, hard to march out of." Not until the 13th century did Afghanistan fall to the Mongols and become part of the Muslim world. But the Afghan fighters remained ferocious when latter-day empires tried to conquer them—the British Empire and now the Soviets. By late afternoon, my bottom was sore and chafed from the friction of bouncing on the horse practically bare backed.

"No more," I told them. "We stop and find a place to sleep."

The next morning, I refused to ride the horse. I packed all the camera gear into my backpack and hijacked Sleepy's bicycle. Exhilarated, I rode ahead of my bodyguards, stopping at each fork in the road for them to catch up. Sleepy grinned when he saw me waiting. These young men reminded me of my kid brother: friendly, fun, and respectful.

Finally, after being on the road for hours, we arrived at the helicopter scene. My bodyguards stood next to the charred fifty-seven-foot long Mi-24, split open and lying sideways. It looked like Moby Dick rising out of the ocean with the tiny hunters dwarfed in its shadow. It turned out that we didn't bring gasoline to fake anything so I shot the scene as a series of still images of a broken helicopter.

But, later, back in New York, I found out that Maria had taken training camp footage to CBS News and passed it off as combat footage. My footage was used to deceive. The ambush scene I shot earlier had been combined with the training footage to look like a bigger battle, with more Afghans fighting than were actually there.

On the return trip, our crew traded the horse for a camel. This time, I sat high up on the camel's back, on a throne piled tall with soft cushions, rocking left and right, moving along steadily for four hours. My first ride on a camel was incomparable to being on a saddleless, stubborn horse.

But it didn't last. At a tea rest stop, we ditched the camel and hijacked a colorful bus with red, orange, and yellow metal cut-outs adorning the windshield frame. Large sacks of grain, stacked three rows tall, were strapped to the roof. My two companions (and their Kalashnikovs) stood in front of the psychedelic bus, while villagers crowded around us. Apparently, the local people were used to having their public transportation being derailed for a few hours. Another short detour for the Afghani cause. Sleepy climbed onto the roof with his bicycle, while Grumpy and I got in. Passengers stared at us. Doc probably would not have approved of our flashy travel methods, which drew unnecessary attention to our activities. We crammed together with caged chickens, tied-up goats, baskets of fruit, and whatever else could be loaded on the bus. After a half hour trip, we stopped the festive bus. The passengers waved goodbye, not the least upset by the surprise commandeering of their vehicle.

* * *

At this point, we were reunited with Doc and the rest of the mujahedeen, who had arrived by motorbike. We sat together outside a nondescript mud house on cotton blankets for our typical diet of greasy lard. Boiled chunks of lamb with inches of fat floated like ocean buoys in thick, oily water. Sleepy started a fire in the deep hearth to bake fresh bread. He patted a ball of dough flat like a pancake and, with a wooden stick, slapped it on the inside wall of the dugout ground. After a few minutes, he grabbed the hot, soft bread, which looked more like Indian chapati than the traditional Afghani flat bread, and offered us the fragrant rolls. With my right hand, I used the yeasty bread to catch the floating lard in the stew. Thankfully, the bread absorbed some of the grease, making it possible to digest.

After dinner, we traveled on, this time in a motorcycle brigade. I rode on the back of the bike, holding on to Doc's waist. He yelled orders to Grumpy to go ahead of us and find a safe place for the night. Then he sped up his bike and didn't look back. Doc embodied the self-confidence of a tribal man who followed his gut, instinctively knowing the dangers of war and how to respond quickly. I was under his rule and protection. Not a soldier nor one of the women in his family but a woman journalist, a third sex that required brand new customs. Doc set himself apart to keep boundaries clear with his men and with me. I didn't question his authority. I felt safe with him.

As I bounced on the back of the motorbike over potholed dirt roads, my backpack repeatedly pounded the metal lens of the Bolex camera in one spot against my back. I was bruised and hurting by the time we finally stopped in front of a Kishmi raisin barn, where Grumpy stood waiting for us. The lens had gashed my back, and the grit from the road seeped under my unwashed tunic.

Through the window slats of the barn, I saw dozens of screens on which thousands of grapes dried into golden raisins. We entered the musty, sweet- raisin-smelling, cavernous space for the night and spread out in rows, barely an arm's length apart. Lying in my sleeping bag, I rubbed the raw, open wound on my back, now infected from the dirt that covered my body everywhere. The coughing and rustling sounds of my companions were comforting and familiar and lulled me to sleep. When I awoke the next morning, the barn was streaming with sun rays piercing through the tiny open slats in the walls, the yellow grapes shining like golden crystals hanging from a chandelier.

I had slept a long time, and now I had a rare moment of privacy. All the men were outside except Doc, who approached me quietly. His patu was casually draped over his shoulder. His face was relaxed, and he was looking at me. I saw his almond-shaped eyes wide and a big smile on his face. We rarely spoke, even though his English was good. I felt like I was one of the guys, though Doc treated me more like a dignitary, but with none of the privileges.

My wound was encrusted with dirt and festering. I could feel pus oozing through the back of my tunic.

"You're hurt?" The commander pointed to the wet spot. He exuded protective masculinity like a lion with his mate. He was close enough that I could smell him, a mixture of fertile earth, gas fuel, and smoke. He touched my back, pausing a moment near the bloody spot. This tenderness aroused me. He opened a first aid kit, took out a bottle of medicinal alcohol, and poured it on a white gauze. I awkwardly wiped the wound. Then, he handed me a bandage to place over the sore. Smiling as I winced, I looked up at his bushy beard and cherub's face, and lingered at his dark brown eyes.

A flash and charge passed through us. The sun streamed through a crack in the rafters, touching our crowns. We kissed, hard, fast. I allowed lust to pull him inside me. He unknotted the rope around his pajama pants and revealed pure nakedness. I straddled him, squatting, as he raised me up and down. The sun overexposed the dust particles surrounding us, as we gasped and exhaled the pulsating rhythm.

It was just this once that we made love. I was startled how my own desire had no boundaries. In this wild Afghani world, where men were soldiers, I found my own wildness, my own strength, and a lustfulness that was mine to do with as I wanted. I wanted sex that matched my strength, courage, and toughness. An electric joy charged and climaxed in me.

CHAPTER 3
A GIFT FROM GOD

Later that day, I wrapped my arms around Doc's tight waist as we motorbiked to his uncle's village. My nose up against his back smelled charcoal smoke—elemental, dark, and rich—dominated my consciousness. My reverie was interrupted when Doc promised me a real Afghani feast. This time, he meant it. Sabaa was today.

I had tasted traditional Afghani food for the first time at Commander Muslim's house, while waiting with Maria to cross the Pakistani border. Day after day and night after night, we were treated to delicately spiced goat stews, vegetables cooked in flavorful sauces, and plenty of fresh baked bread. The food had been the highlight of our long and boring days. The prospect of relaxing in a real home, with a meal like that again, made my stomach growl in anticipation.

In the Pashtun village, I saw tall dirt walls on either side of the road hiding entire domestic worlds. Every five hundred feet was a large, hand-carved wooden door, which, when opened, revealed a courtyard and, sometimes, several buildings housing the family clan. It was a big risk for Doc to bring me to his family. A young cousin might gossip with a neighbor about my visit. Spies were every-where—helping both sides. Most information was based on rumors and could either help someone gain favor with the Soviets or support the Afghani cause. If the Soviets, or the communist-based Afghan government, learned of anyone helping the mujahedeen, the devastation would be immediate and brutal. Their family, along with other villagers, could be killed. Survivors might end up at a sewage-filled refugee camp in Pakistan. Or an individual could be taken to Kabul to be tortured, as Dopey was.

Doc wanted to show me how he had lived before the war. His own home was in another village, further away, but he retreated at his uncle's when he needed a break from the front lines. He was proud of his heritage. According to Afghan hospitality and cultural code, a guest is a gift from God. I would be the guest of honor. Even when there was little material wealth, a household would do its best to share whatever they had with a visitor. They might spend all their savings on a meal with meat to fulfill this cultural obligation.

We entered through a green carved door and into a vast courtyard, where the last surviving fruits of fall, pomegranates and apples, hung on the branches of trees like Christmas ornaments. A smiling boy, about eight, dressed in a pressed tunic, dropped the baby goat he was holding, ran up to Doc, and wrapped his thin arms around Doc's thighs. Doc took the boy's embroidered cap from his head and rubbed his fluffy hair. The boy giggled. Doc slapped his narrow back, and they both laughed. In the corner of the garden courtyard, three women with colorful scarves draped around their heads, gold jewelry hanging from their ears, and bangles on their arms, squatted, scooping Afghani goat stew from wide-open black metal pots.

Doc brought me into the living room, a large hall where two men in their fifties and an older man in his seventies were gathered. Shelves carved out of the dirt walls were lined with pink and red floral scarves. Two baroque vases stood on the shelves. A tribal rug, with intricate patterns of orange and blue geometric flowers, covered the floor of the whole room where the men were seated. They leaned on black and white zebra pattern cushions against one side of the wall.

"Assalamu alaikum," peace be to you, Doc's two middle-aged uncles greeted me. They wore bright white tunics and pants, gold embroidered vests, and matching caps on their white heads. Their faces were framed by long white beards. Children followed, wiggling on their elders' heels, beaming. A shy girl hung on her grandfather's leg, trying to catch a furtive glimpse of me. A boy jumped boldly onto the cushion, then landed seated and cross-legged.

A very old man with a deeply wrinkled face, old enough to be Doc's grandfather, sat on the floor, in front of the pale green sheet where the meal would be served. Of the women, I saw only their hands, delicately jingling from bracelets swiftly moving through the curtained doorway, passing the bowls to the children, who brought dish after dish of steamy white rice, cooked goat in tomato sauce, chopped greens, eggplant in yogurt, cheese with raisins, and long flatbread. With each dish I was lulled and taken on a caravan of spices: paprika, saffron, cardamom, mint, coriander, pickled lemon, rose water … The men chatted in Pashto about the war, births, deaths, sickness, and weddings, letting me go deeper into my own thoughts. I felt as though their stories were like ballads, timeless stories told over eons, so different from my grandparents' ritual of watching TV after dinner.

Doc cut open a dark red fruit with ruby seeds and handed me a few seeds to chew on. The tart nectar touched my tongue and bubbles erupted in my mouth, better than any French champagne. Afterwards, the pomegranate became a fruit that I would forever crave. Green tea, poured into etched glasses and served on polished brass trays, interrupted the Pashto conversation.

Doc translated a question from the uncle with mischievous brown eyes, "Do you have husband?"

I shook my head no. They laughed heartily from their bellies, which were full from the dinner.

"My fiancé is in Greece doing military service."

Doc translated for his family first, children listening, too. Then for me. "Your father get many, many fat sheep for you. Maybe camel, too," said the second uncle, with bushy white eyebrows and a long, mullah-style beard. I stared down at my cup of tea and picked out a pattern on the Oriental rug that looked like birds on a tree. Marriage seemed to be about captivity here. Home was a closed world and the men were the guards. Women were chattel in this society. They found their individuality among each other in a domestic world.

There was more laughing.

I asked the first uncle, "How many wives do you have?"

His eyes brightened, and he held up four fingers, the maximum number allowed under Islamic law—something I first read about in my guidebook. I turned to look at Doc, who avoided my stare.

I returned to the conversation about my future husband, "Only if I can be number 1 wife. I won't share."

We all laughed at my adamant requirement for marriage. Doc smiled at me for an instant, and I met his eyes, the secret of our liaison dissolving between us. Had I been a Muslim fiancée and the head mullah found out about our affair, I could have been stoned. Doc, on the other hand, would hardly have suffered a blemish on his reputation. My guidebook was full of these cultural adages.

In Quetta, before crossing the Afghan border, Maria and I had stayed at the tribal chief's compound, waiting for arms to be secured. Commander Muslim had four wives. During the day, a constant circus of emotions swirled around us. The first wife, the senior matriarch by twenty years, often stormed through the house barking demands at her three younger rivals, who were the same age as her married daughter. Each night, the wives waited in anticipation as the patriarch chose which bedroom he would enter. The matriarch tried to ignore this ritual, already resigned to the fact that she would be overlooked. The youngest wife, with a newborn suckling at her breast, seemed grateful not to be chosen. The other two wives peeked out of their rooms, eyeing each other in a staring contest. Then, the fateful slam of the door followed.

* * *

My mother had wanted it all, the career, the husband, the family, and it was a disaster. In the fifties, the woman was expected to support her husband by staying home and taking care of the children—not so different from tribal Afghani customs. But my mother was different. She wanted to be free and in control of her destiny. She was smart and ambitious. But the reality proved to be too hard for her. After witnessing her struggle, I didn't believe it was possible to succeed on all fronts. Something would have to be sacrificed.

I wanted a chance to be a filmmaker and to be with George. He made incessant marriage proposals. I conceded to marry him some time in the future. I was determined that our life together would not be under any of the cultural rules of our parents' generation. We would have to find equality, openness, better communication, and ways to work out difficulties. I had no idea how we would succeed. I had no role models.

I had promised marriage to George, after he agreed on an open relationship.

* * *

Behind the curtained doorway, rustling sounds caught my attention. An angel-faced teenage girl entered like a ballerina. She tiptoed over to me, took my hand and pulled me up to float off stage into the secret women's quarters. In a second smaller living room, the remains of the women's segregated feast were littered on another dark red Afghani rug. An old woman grinned a toothless smile and patted the pillow next to her for me to sit. More sweet tea was served with store-bought almond cookies on French china. I was full, but could not refuse this graciousness.

Ten women of all ages, from teens to seventies, their faces framed in colorful scarves, circled me. This reminded me of the women's empowerment groups I'd seen in my youth, where the next exercise, falling backwards into their arms, was meant to teach me to trust them. The leader of the group, a woman my mother's age, wearing a bulky tribal silver lapis lazuli necklace, pushed forward and kindly wrapped a floral scarf around my unwashed hair and my face like a veil. A dark-haired toddler, wrapped in her Auntie's arms, reached out and touched my greasy hair. The ballerina girl then escorted me up a rickety wooden staircase that led to the second floor.

The dusk-lit attic room was completely bare, except for two large aluminum metal basins. Women brought large blackened kettles and poured cleansing hot water into the tubs. My ballerina friend ceremoniously removed the veil and lifted my stained tunic over my head. I removed my filthy pants, bra, and panties in a trancelike state and then stepped into the steamy bath, my curves and nakedness exposed to admirers. The Afghan aunties fussed over me, dipping a soft cloth into the divine water that smelled of rose petals and removing layers of grime and dirt from my travels with the mujahedeen.

The Auntie who gave me the scarf opened a sweet-smelling bottle of Clairol shampoo and washed my hair. Silently, she poured pitchers of hot water over me in a matriarchal baptism of women honoring women. This harem rite fit for a queen was my Afghan legacy from ancient Islamic times. Twenty-four hours was all the time we would spend in this oasis.

I felt comfortable traveling with the mujahedeen, they were becoming my friends; but with the circle of women, I could be myself—fragile, vulnerable—and this gave me more strength to go back into the men's world.

* * *

My mother's home had not been a nurturing place. There was no female bonding or support. My mother was depressed, rageful, and stuck in an alcohol addiction. My mother had a fascination with suicide. She told stories about her friend and college roommate, Sylvia Plath. Sylvia Plath was an icon in our home. As a teenager, I recited lines from Sylvia's poem, "The Disquieting Muses," when I walked across D.C.'s Duke Ellington bridge: "And this is the kingdom you bore me to/ Mother, mother. But no frown of mine/ Will betray the company I keep." It was a salve for feelings I tried to process. Sylvia described her windows blown out by a hurricane, "But those ladies broke the panes." Sylvia's pain was an outlet for my unconscious pain. Her witches haunted me and my mother.

When my mother threatened to kill herself one summer, just as I had returned from film school, I allowed myself to be manipulated. My sister Elena and I were held hostage. The threat of my mother killing herself kept us on a vigil that we could not walk away from. We thought of Sylvia and how she didn't mean to kill herself, according to what our mother told us. We were paralyzed by a fear that our mother might kill herself if we didn't do as she told us.

"Missy and Elena, clean the couch now." My mother slurred her words after a fifth of vodka, a fateful command—"Clean!" Elena and

I stared at this yellow mass, squeezed in the tiny space between the three living room walls. The oversized, bright yellow plush corduroy couch was the only item from our family home that my mother had taken to her new place after the divorce.

"Mom, it clearly says to seek professional services and under no circumstances wash the couch yourself," I insisted, staring at her from under the seat cushion—this was obviously a bad idea.

"I don't care! Wash that couch now!"

"We can't. You'll be mad," Elena said.

"Do what I say. I've had enough with you two never listening to me."

Elena and I were used to her tirades and had defied her for most of our teenage years. Then, my mother articulated every word softly, "If you don't clean this couch now, I will kill myself."

We froze. Something in the way she said it made us believe her. My mother passed out and slept on the yellow couch. We didn't leave her. Hours passed, nothing happened. We were on a night watch.

Through the night I watched, as I went back and forth between thoughts of being a prisoner and those of a free person. I decided that I could not protect my mother from herself. If she was destined to kill herself, all I could do was save my sister and me from this psychodrama. In the morning, Elena and I were exhausted and still sure my mother was capable of suicide.

"You, young ladies, defied me. I asked you for a simple chore. Are you going to clean the couch or not?"

I no longer cared if she killed herself. That was up to her. She could not threaten us anymore.

"All right," I said. I went to the kitchen, took out the bucket and filled it with hot water, and grabbed two sponges and a can of Comet. Elena and I scrubbed that damn couch—poured the blue-green powder and soaked the paste into the cushions, releasing the Comet clean smell. We destroyed that yellow couch and left the house.

The yellow couch incident, and many others, prompted me to finally leave. I had wanted to be thousands of miles away from my mother so I chose to move to England after high school. Ironically, I studied film in Covent Garden, the same neighborhood where my mother studied economics. But, on each return visit, I still could get sucked into her volatility, her passion for chaos and negativity. We were stuck in a pattern, and neither of us could find a way out.

* * *

It was near the end of the trip. I had been inside Afghanistan for three weeks—and the war footage was due to CBS in less than ten days. Doc drove me on his motorbike to the same paved road twenty miles west of the Afghan ambush where I had shot the attack on the Soviet convoy. Sleepy and Dopey followed us on a second motorbike. The roar of the two bikes and dust blasted around us in broad daylight.

A new Afghani Commander, Razik, arrived with his own convoy of three Soviet trucks, stolen from an earlier raid, and fresh recruits from the villages. It was time to say goodbye to Doc, Sleepy, and Dopey. With no fanfare, Dopey and Sleepy waved to me as they drove off. Doc parked his bike behind a wall leading to an open dry field that hid us from the main road where Razik and his trucks were waiting for me.

"Be careful," Doc told me. This was the first time we were alone since we made love.

"Nothing will happen to me," I said. "I'm sure of it."

He gave me a gift wrapped in a floral scarf, a silver necklace with a lapis lazuli inlay, which I still wear on special occasions. In exchange, I handed him a pearl bracelet, a good luck charm that I carried in my camera bag. I asked him to please give the jewelry to his wife, who was related to the women who bathed me. With this gift, I hoped to alleviate some of the guilt I felt about our affair.

"Assalamu alaikum," peace be to you, I said. We didn't hug.

"Wa alaikum assalam wa rahmatu Allah." And to you be peace together with God's mercy.

It was a formal Islamic greeting now used for a farewell.

* * *

Commander Razik wanted to take a shortcut on the Kandahar-Herat highway where the Soviet caravan had been attacked a few weeks ago. It was a direct route to take me across the Pakistani border. We passed the broken storehouses that were bombed in the ambush I had shot earlier in the month. The paved road felt open, vulnerable, and too quiet on this early afternoon. The sun was falling behind the distant hills with pinkish orange clouds in the sky. Razik pulled the trucks off the road for the mujahedeen to pray.

Back on the paved road, dark shadows covered the large rock formations in the distance. I was listening to the rumble of the truck, the speedometer climbing to 60 km/h on the flat road. We were moving at a steady pace, nearly reaching the rocks before the mountains ahead. Then Razik stopped again. Something snapped in me. Some kind of intuition, a demand from a higher sense of awareness, urged me to follow through, even though it made no sense.

I felt like a maniac as I yelled, over and over, "I want to be home for Christmas!" The Afghans had no idea what I was screaming about. Nor did I. Sure, Christmas was seven days away, and I wanted to be home for Christmas. Some of my best memories were opening presents around the Christmas tree, but my family was dispersed now, and there really wasn't a family home to go home to for the holidays. I wanted to bring Dan Rather the footage on time, too, and I knew it would be close. It was at least five days from the Afghanistan border to D.C., if I caught every flight on time and there were no delays. But, really...

The five tall, bearded, muscular mujahedeen, who could have been brothers, looked up at me from their kneeling positions, frozen, perhaps wondering if I was possessed. My words were having no impact. Christmas. Home. The most rugged of the men recited his prayers in the familiar whisper, bowing to Allah. I shoved him full force. Caught off guard, he toppled over and then stood up, stunned. I kept pushing him towards the truck. Razik and the other men followed. They stopped mid-prayer and drove off.

My breath, normal again, was deep and relaxed; I was almost giddy during the smooth ride on the paved road out of Afghanistan. When we got close to the Pakistan border, four shadows in the distance walked towards the trucks. These Afghani mujahedeen recognized us and started running, shouting, "Wadareja!" STOP!

We pulled over again. All of the men jumped out of the trucks. I followed. Talking fast and with wild gesticulations, all nine men turned to face me. One stranger pointed at me. More talking, as though I had stumbled into a foreign movie with no subtitles—something big had happened, I just didn't know what. Then, one of the brothers kneeled on the ground and prayed in my direction like I was Mecca. Now, I really had no idea what was going on. Another mujahedeen copied the first one. Soon, the gang was honoring me. Eventually, I realized what had happened: The mujahedeen who had stopped us had just mined the road, not expecting any comrades to drive through at night. Had we arrived a few minutes later, we would have all been blown up. My intuition and my outrageous action had saved us.

Strangely, I didn't feel attached to life or death, but I felt protected, driven by an invisible force. Nothing made sense. This journey into war in Afghanistan could have been a death fall, but the experiences I was going through made me feel energized and unbreakable.

Yet I had volunteered to be part of a violent act, filming the caravan ambush that most likely resulted in more deaths from Soviet retaliation. Decades later, I would take the Bodhisattva vow to do no harm. But in Afghanistan, I said no prayers for any of us, not the mujahedeen, not the villagers, not even myself. At the time, I hadn't wondered if Doc would have attacked that Soviet convoy had I not been there to record the event. How much of guerrilla warfare was done for publicity? I was there to do a job, record what was happening. I was supposed to be the journalist. "Just the facts." But, instead, I rooted for this tribe, their cause, and I came to believe that I had contributed in a small way to perpetuating the killing.

* * *

It was the dead of night, a bright full moon lay flat against the black sky. My backpack, with all my camera gear and finished reels of film, was thrown in the trunk of a sedan. I was back in Quetta, and a taxi driver opened the back door, chauffeur-like, to take me to the Karachi International airport. I climbed in. Millions of stars pierced through the pitch black darkness. The vastness of the universe enveloped me. The driver pushed his foot on the gas pedal to the floor. We were off like a sonic rocket. Flying through the desert night, we drove through the Chiltan mountains to cross deeper into Pakistan. I was on my way home. The driver turned the wheel sharp right, then sharp left, hydroplaning on the gravel. As the sun rose, an ecstatic mystery took me to the Divine. This kind of awakening could have happened after years of meditation or during a near death experience, but in my case, it occurred after I took the risk of my life and went into the unknown by myself, with a group of men. I stretched myself beyond my habitual comfort zones. Grace descended. I was shot with a blissfulness that stunned me. I had opened myself fully to what is, in all its glories and difficulties.

The tip of the sun unveiled and softened the sky. The huge ball of flame diffused the blackness. I could feel every cell flickering inside me. My body dissolved into the light. There was no me, no car, no driver, no mountain, no sunrise. I was exploding, bouncing, containing all. I was it. This oneness was all there was. There were no boundaries, no time, just this. The sensation was startlingly palpable.

This ecstatic moment was a gift that opened possibilities. I now felt that life was about more than constant anxiety, survival, and the pursuit of personal goals. I discovered a new truth: There is an existence infused with a divine quality that is inspiring, awesome, and life-transforming.

SECOND PART

ENDURANCE THROUGH STRUGGLE

"The creation of something new is not accomplished by the intellect
but by the play instinct acting from inner necessity."

~ C. G. Jung

CHAPTER 4

PANJSHIR VALLEY OR BUST

"It'll be a big story," said John, calling from London to invite me on a new assignment to Afghanistan. "Dan Rather will probably want in on it. I already have interest from the BBC," John concluded his pitch.

"I'll do it," I fired back without hesitation. And, in that moment, all my plans changed 180 degrees.

John, the British journalist who, with Maria and my fiancé George, had initiated the first trip into Afghanistan, had tracked down my phone number from George. He had caught the broadcast of the Soviet ambush that I had shot in Afghanistan eight months earlier on the BBC and was favorably impressed. He now wanted me to go back into Afghanistan to cover the alleged cease-fire in the Panjshir Valley, for the fourth anniversary of the Soviet invasion.

After returning home from Afghanistan, I moved to New York City to be an independent filmmaker. I quickly gravitated to a community of like-minded artists and filmmakers in downtown Manhattan, which included Sarah Peterson, a fellow filmmaker and artist ten years older than me. A few months earlier, in June 1983, I marched with Sarah at the International Day of Nuclear Disarmament in protest of the Cold War arms race. I was helping her produce *Big Red*, a daring film about her eight-day journey on the Trans-Siberian railroad in 1980, during the Olympic boycott. At a time when Americans thought the Soviets were evil, Sarah wanted to show that peace was possible between American and Soviet citizens.

My money from the Afghanistan assignment was running out. I had stretched out the $3,000 as long as I could. I would need a paying job or at least a part-time gig to pay the rent. John's plan was to get the story and be back in time for the broadcast on December 27, 1983, which was only four months away. So, going back to Afghanistan was a chance to use my previous experience to produce a news story about this unique situation in the region, a rare peaceful strategy during the escalating Cold War tension. I thought this story could make Western leaders pay attention, maybe even change their policies toward Afghanistan, and hopefully do some good. It was also a way to make a lot of money quickly.

After a few days of preparation, I called my father, who adamantly pleaded with me not to go, "It's in the second round of duty that soldiers are more likely to be killed. The first time you can count on beginner's luck." My father didn't fight in Vietnam. He told me he was honorably discharged from the Air Force when he threatened to go public about Americans targeting civilians.

Then I called my mother, who breezily wished me a safe trip. The last time it was the other way around, my father encouraged me and my mother tried to stop me. As usual, my parents never agreed on anything. By now, they were divorced, so their disagreement didn't cause the usual static, it simply offered me antagonistic points of view to weigh and channel into my own decisions.

We managed to win two contracts, BBC for the United Kingdom broadcast rights and CBS for the United States rights. John had been right. Dan Rather, the only major news anchorman in the U.S. to cross the border into Afghanistan, wanted an exclusive for the CBS Evening News. We would travel through the Hindu Kush to the Panjshir Valley, further north from Kandahar in the Parwan Province and near the foothills of the Himalayas. I would interview Commander Massoud about the cease fire he negotiated with the Soviet government. Massoud was a hero for the Afghans, a high commander, who strategized political solutions outside of traditional tribal rules enforced by the local mullahs. He was neither afraid to rule inside the country nor to fight alongside his men.

It was the fall of 1983. Going back into a war zone with a better understanding of its complexities could be a chance to have a positive impact. The Soviets were not evil, and peace could be a possibility in Afghanistan. I felt I had an opportunity to relieve suffering. The unbiased reporter was a myth. There was always a point of view, an individual perspective, and the more up front I was about my own perspective, the more honest I felt I could be about the story I was telling.

* * *

John sat tall and looked around the garden pavilion, where pink roses grew upright in rectangular hedges. At Dean's Hotel, where we were staying, we were surrounded by ex-pats.

"This is your third cigarette before breakfast," I told him.

"Silly woman."

I had been counting his cigarettes, an attempt at rationing. Our cash was running out. We had been stuck in Peshawar for a couple weeks, waiting for a mujahedeen group to take us into Afghanistan. We were counting on an American journalist, Ed Girardet, who made it his business to know all sorts of ins and outs in Afghanistan. Having spent years covering the region for the Christian Science Monitor, he was the reporter most trusted by the mujahedeen. John knew him from his first trip in Kandahar. Ed made the introductions for us to meet the leaders of the Jamiat Group in Pakistan, one of the most powerful of the mujahedeen groups. Ahmad Shah Massoud was their major commander in Afghanistan. However, we were facing one delay after another. Each contact at the Jamiat Group kept telling us to come back tomorrow. "Farda," they told us in Dari, a local Persian dialect.

John and I continued to pick at the toast and marmalade in front of us, while drinking English Breakfast tea. We took all our meals now at the hotel because we could charge them to room service.

Many years ago, Rudyard Kipling and Sir Winston Churchill had stayed at this rustic, sherbet green Victorian hotel, a colonial oasis in the center of Peshawar, a 2,500-year-old living city. The Pakistani border town was overcrowded by Afghan refugees, as well as government, military, and NGO officials from various countries that had a stake in the Afghani war.

This was a very different Pakistani town from the one Maria and I had been stuck in during our first trip. And this hotel was a far cry from Muslim's house with his four wives. At that time, the only fresh air we were allowed was in his walled-in courtyard or on the roof of his house. This time, it was a lot more fun. There were bars in Peshawar hotels, where John and I could have a beer and exchange war stories with other journalists from Europe, even some Americans. The men had this tough, macho quality, much like the way John carried himself. Yet only John, Girardet, and I had been in battles. Most of the other journalists who bragged about their stories had mainly filmed refugee camps and interviewed officials in hotel lobbies.

I felt like I had earned my stripes after my footage was broadcast on BBC and CBS. I was one of the boys, a member of the war journalism club. I heard rumors that there were other women journalists, but I never saw them. At 22 years old, I was also one of the youngest filmmakers there.

"The Soviets were so stupid to invade. Don't they know the history?" said John. "The British Empire tried to conquer Afghanistan. The tribal leaders extorted higher and higher bribes from General Willoughby Cotton, head of the British mission at the time, but when her Majesty cut all the funds, the Afghans stormed the fort. This was the winter of 1841, and the British soldiers, civilians, even children were forced to travel through the harsh mountains. The same ones we're going to climb to reach the Pansjshir Valley."

He loved to tell the same story over and over …

"Over 16,000 Brits were murdered in this terrible massacre, all of them retreating through the narrow mountain pass trying to get out of Afghanistan. Only one man, surgeon Wolfgang Brydon, survived the death march and described what had happened when he finally made it to Jalalabad," he added.

"Fools," concluded John, as we finished breakfast. In his mind, if the British couldn't conquer the Afghans, nobody else could. Then he lit up another cigarette, as if to defy me. "Fifth fag this morning," he said.

I ordered a fizzy fresh lemonade from a Pakistani waiter in a red tailored jacket. I enjoyed the refreshing drink. It reminded me of the comforts of the colonial times, as I imaged them to be.

"Are you sure your grandmother didn't have an affair with a Raj?" I asked, wanting to lighten the mood. And I knew John liked the teasing. He had told me how he was one of the darker ones in his family and that maybe it had something to do with his grandparents being stationed in India.

"Wanker."

I wasn't sure if he was talking about me or his grandmother's lover. He didn't deny the possibility, which didn't make it true. Regardless, his love for Imperial Britain and its history lived in his bones.

John was not my type. At times, he struck me as too full of himself, in a British sort of way. John had postponed his wedding with Rose, his fiancé, after it became clear we would not be back in time. Getting to the Panjshir Valley was proving to be difficult. We were no closer to getting in than when we first arrived.

Two single beds were pulled apart from their customary couple's bed in the one room we shared to save money. There was a ceiling fan and a Western toilet, two nice amenities. After a few weeks of living in close quarters together, we were becoming more and more dependent on each other, and we didn't know how long we could keep this up. We were a bit competitive for attention and who knew more—more like bickering siblings than professional colleagues.

John was fascinated by Commander Massoud, a mythical character, "The Lion of Panjshir," as he was called. Massoud was young, only in his late 20s. Ed Girardet had told us he didn't speak English, only French, and had this strange gesture with his shoulder, a kind of twitch. I wanted to see what he was talking about.

Rumors had it that Massoud was influenced by Sun Tzu's *The Art of War*, especially the idea that war requires quick and appropriate responses to changing conditions. He was not like the other tribal leaders, who rode around Pakistan in air-conditioned Land Rovers that were paid for by governments who had a stake in the war outcome, or the fat old tribal leaders, as John called them, who lived safely in Peshawar. This was 1983, before the American public knew anything about the U.S. funding the mujahedeen or providing military aid against the Soviets in an attempt to escalate the war.

I had learned my lesson in Kandahar and wanted a news story that did not involve staging any battles for the sake of the media. This cease-fire story promised to open the possibility that the West could leverage their power to influence the Soviets to negotiate, spread the cease-fire to the rest of the country, and hopefully stop the war and all the killing.

* * *

Two weeks earlier, John and I had flown via British Airways, paid for by the BBC, and had arrived in Islamabad in the middle of the night. The capital's airport was cleaner and more orderly than Karachi's airport, where Maria and I had arrived the previous year. Situated at a higher elevation, it was not as hot or humid. John and I paced, as the porters brought the baggage to the waiting area. We were standing alone, the last to leave the party. John's suitcase, with over four hours of Super 8 film, was missing. The Elmo Super 8 camera, efficient, light, and easy to use, would be of no use if we didn't have the film stock.

"Look at my wife, she's distraught. This is meant to be our honeymoon," John lied to the British Airways manager.

"Our plans are ruined," I faked tears. One night in an Islamabad hotel could cost more than a week in Peshawar. I was in charge of the budget, including the cash advance from CBS for hotels and other sundries. I had estimated we had enough money for two to three weeks while we made our contacts to get inside Afghanistan.

Sympathetic, the Brit winked at John, "Don't worry chap. We'll sort out this mess."

"An American airline would never be this generous," I whispered to John, as we checked into a four-star hotel. We were given free room service and a stipend to buy new clothes, while they looked for our lost bag. In spite of this luxurious treatment, we were anxious to leave for Peshawar.

Four days later, British Airways found our bag and an excuse— something about it falling off the conveyer belt at Heathrow Airport, and then some more difficulties in sending it to us in Islamabad. What incompetence! Ready to go to Peshawar, the frontier town, we hailed a taxi and rode two hours to our destination. On the outskirts of Peshawar, we saw grey tents pitched across the horizon on the treeless expanse of red land. Immense refugee camps were set up by the Red Cross, their red and white flags heralding meager hope for the families who escaped the battles of the war.

I wore my Afghani green pants and tunic from my first trip to Kandahar, although it didn't seem necessary for me to hide my identity. There were Westerners dressed in jeans, khaki pants, and skirts, who were aid workers from NGOs or journalists from different news agencies. Pakistani police officers directed traffic at nearly every corner. I could walk without harassment on these busy streets. John and I visited the markets and hotel lobbies, where we met journalists who had the same purpose as we did: to convince a mujahedeen group to take them across the border, only a few hours drive away.

In our first few days in Peshawar, John and I jumped into a rickshaw with directions to the Jamiat headquarters from Ed Girardet. John bumped his head on the rickshaw's yellow awning, designed for much shorter men. The rickshaw stopped on a residential street in front of an open sewer, where children played with a deflated soccer ball. I covered my nose and mouth with my patu to avoid the shitty smell. We entered one of the two-story, nondescript cement houses with cracked walls.

The Jamiat leaders gave us the VIP treatment: tea, biscuits, and the promise that we would leave for Afghanistan with one of their mujahedeen groups, as soon as the arms arrived. If we wanted to get the real story, not a quick border news piece, we had to be both persistent and patient.

So we climbed into our rickshaw to return to the hotel, when a short, round-faced, twenty-year-old Pakistani man jumped in next to John. He assured us he was there to help us, to be our translator. John accepted this arrangement. I was suspicious.

There was something about this man's forwardness that I did not like. John got a cheap thrill at my annoyance. Each day, this man stalked us outside the hotel. He would wait beside the iron gate and signal a rickshaw to come over to the entrance the moment we appeared. John allowed him to join us when we traveled to the Jamiat office for the daily report. We kept thinking we would be leaving tomorrow. But tomorrow turned into weeks. John liked having the man tag along with us, when we went to the markets, toured the city, and hung out at tea shops. John even made him his caddy when he played golf at a nearby course built during the colonial rule. He would only leave us when we went into the hotel bars where the foreigners mingled.

This man leered at me. His mustache was neatly trimmed. Each day he would get bolder and bolder, pretending to bump into me, then grazing my back with his small hand. One morning, he tried to sit next to me in the rickshaw. I pushed John in the middle, and he enjoyed this skirmish. John slid over and enabled his caddy to sit next to me. He placed his smelly arm around my shoulders like we were a couple. I shoved it off. Then he cupped my breast nearest to him. I yelled at him. John laughed, which encouraged him. As I got out of the vehicle, his fingernails swept over my butt.

I found this unwanted male attention demeaning and confusing. However, John was convinced this guy was our chance, our only chance, to get inside Afghanistan. After five weeks of waiting in Peshawar and going to the Jamiat office every day, I took my frustrations out on John. I was mad at him, about his damn cigarettes that cost more than a dinner out, about our unpaid hotel bill, and about letting this guy harass me all the time. And I told him so.

John was tired of my nagging. He left me at the hotel while he and the Pakistani guy went to the post office, where there was an international pay phone. He called the BBC office and asked the producer to wire four hundred English pounds. The producer offered to send five hundred pounds, enough to cover the hotel bill and all our meals. Then they went to the Jamiat office to discuss a new plan. Our contacts there offered to have us travel with a caravan to Istalif, then to the Panjshir Valley. Not our first choice. We had wanted a direct route to Commander Massoud. Now it would be a race between when the money would arrive and when we got the signal to leave for Afghanistan.

John brought the Pakistani guide into our hotel room. It was the first time. The Pakistani guy slithered close to me waiting to have his moment. He took credit for our change of plans and told me that going to Istalif was the solution we were waiting for. He sat close to me, too close next to me on my bed, his nasty breath in my left ear. His torso pinned me against the headboard. He was stronger than expected for his light frame. His hands were on my shoulder, pulling his face close to mine. I pushed him off and whined for John to get this guy out of the room.

Instead, John left the room. The lech embraced me. I felt disgusted by his attention. I felt pressured by his sexual overtures. I moved to the chair. He stared at me. Then, without saying a word, he knelt in front of me and put his head in my lap. I felt shame. I stood up and moved back to the bed. He followed me, leaned against me, held me down while he took off his pants.

I could have screamed, scratched him, bit him. Instead, I let him enter me and then shoved him out the door. This was the first time a man persisted, forced himself on me, didn't take my Nos. I had been coerced, and my lack of boundaries had allowed this sex to take place. I was more used to not being wanted, too fat for American men. I felt vulnerable. I allowed my boundary to be broken by a man who wanted what he wanted. The act was a form of manipulation. I had whored myself to get inside Afghanistan. My shock at what happened produced a numbness that made me feel I was still in control.

***

The next day the Pakistani guy arranged for a taxi driver, a cousin of his, to take us to Parachinar, the last Pakistani town before the no-man's land bordering Afghanistan. The BBC money came through just in time, and we paid our hotel debt. The following day we would be uniting with the mujahedeen caravan in Teri Mangal, a makeshift village before the mountain pass, where the men were packing thirty or more horses with ammunition, metal boxes of three-inch metal bullets, and a few large boxes with rocket launchers. John and I would be hiking with our gear on our backs. We couldn't afford horses, which would have made our trip much easier.

One thing John and I were in agreement about: We didn't want to shoot a battle. We were looking for a deeper story, not just sexy bang-bang footage. We wanted to understand how one commander negotiated peace with the Soviets. We would film the Panjshir village at peace and Massoud, a mujahedeen commander out in the open conducting business with the villagers. Margaret Mead had said that one small group of thoughtful, committed citizens could change the world. I believed this to be true, and Massoud's story would prove it.

Despite the sexual harassment, I knew my purpose here. I saw my role on this trip very differently from my first trip to Afghanistan. Before, I was interested in being the eyewitness, but this time, I believed in the message and thought it would make a difference. I had an obligation. I also felt uniquely qualified for the assignment—I was a competent filmmaker, had the trust of the mujahedeen from my previous success, and spoke French, which meant I could communicate directly with Massoud. Above all, I wanted to produce and broadcast this story internationally.

John and I arranged to stay at the taxi driver's home in Parachinar overnight. The next morning, he would get us to Teri Mangal, a dangerous job for any driver, with over thirty police checkpoints to cross, where we might be stopped and detained. We only had $100 left. The driver wanted $30, or over 1500 rupees, a generous sum, worth more than two months' wages at the time.

***

The driver had me sleep in the women's quarters, on a large bed, alone, in a big room. John was with the men on the other side of the house. I had trouble sleeping that night. Lying in the large bed under the red floral cotton comforter, I thought about being 16 years old in Wyoming. I was rock climbing a sheer cliff, a four-day hike away from any road. A thick, purple nylon rope was fixed in a figure eight knot to my harness. The rope passed through the climbing protection anchored into the rock and down to my belayer, the person responsible for my safety if I fell. I wore my $70 rubber toed climbing shoes, purchased from babysitting money. I began to climb flat against the rock, like the coyote in the Road Runner cartoon. I breathed granite and focused on narrow cracks in the rock, where my toe would fit as my fingers grasped for any possible hold.

I was the chubby girl, moving up invisible stairs in the mountain face, no fancy reaches or legs swinging over her head pulling the rest of her body up. I was nothing like the monkey boys who scampered up rocks, defying gravity. No, I had to manifest steps with handholds, so I would have to take a new route never tried before. By sheer imagination and determination, I slowly reached the top of the cliff.

One time I slipped. My error had been big. I had taken a 45 degree angle swing and was not fully protected. I fell in a pendulum motion 20 feet down and smashed my ankle against the rock. The metal hooks attached to the crevices of the rocks were meant to keep the falls at a short distance, as long as I only stayed on the course leading to the summit. I hiked out for four days on that injured ankle and never went rock climbing again. I hoped nothing similar would happen on this trip.

Crossing the border would be an endurance test. I would have to keep up with these men. There was no turning back. Tomorrow, I would be crossing the Hindu Kush, some of the highest peaks in the world. I had reassured the mujahedeen that I could climb. But how could I compare with these men? They were like goats, running up and down these mountains their whole lives.

The next morning, I woke up in the taxi driver's house with a body next to me. A young boy was touching me, his hand between my legs. I screamed, "Get off! Get out!" I was so furious, so fed up with these men who knew no boundaries. But this sexual advance came from a boy, who could not have been more than 11 years old. This was disgusting. I shouted at him, "What is your problem?"

His younger sister ran into the room. She was sobbing, asking me what had happened. I wanted to punish the boy. His sister was crying uncontrollably, more disturbed than me by her brother's presence in my room. I took some deep breaths to calm myself. I ushered both of them out of the room. Then I sat up in the bed, pulled the cover up to my chin, and waited until morning arrived.

I was not going to let any man or boy take advantage of me after what happened with the lecherous guide in Peshawar. And the girl's reaction had seemed too intense. Was this boy touching his sister inappropriately? I didn't tell anyone at the time. I needed this boy's father to drive us to Teri Mangal.

In the morning, I wore a large purple chador, a fabric bag covering my body, meant to protect women from men's desires. The sack made me uninteresting to the opposite sex, uninviting, unappealing, and unisexual. Yet, in this case, it would also hide my American identity from the Pakistani police at the checkpoints. I stepped out of the taxi driver's house, tripped over the fabric, and fell face down in the mud. John had grown a beard and wore a turban over his dark hair, Sikh-like, to disguise himself. We made it past all the checkpoints and arrived at the mujahedeen camp without any trouble.

The driver asked for double his fare. We argued but in the end gave him $60, which left us only $40. The caravan would be leaving the following night. There would be few places to spend any money, once we were in Afghanistan. We could count on the mujahedeen to feed us, but I didn't like that we were so broke.

Teri Mangal was a dirty place, full of steep dirt roads, makeshift camps with tents, and a few simple mud structures. Here, we met four French doctors from the Médecins Sans Frontières. France sent their young, bright doctors to do community service all over the world; some doctors chose places for their possibility of adventure. One of them was a blond woman, cute, fragile, and delicate. She looked like she would be more accustomed to drinking a café au lait at a Paris cafe than walking around in this dangerous, muddy place.

"C'est incroyable tu cherche pour Massoud," the French woman said to me, in awe of our search for Massoud.

"Oui, c'est vrais. John et moi veux faire la connaissance de Massoud," I said—it's true we want to meet him. She was impressed by my French and especially by my accent. I told her the story of how in kindergarten my French teacher had taken me for private lessons in the girls' bathroom, where she had instructed me how to gargle water so I would sound the French "r" in the proper way. My mother had insisted I learn French. She abhorred how Americans didn't know a second language and had registered me at L'École Française, where I was the only native-born English-speaking child. I felt out of my element, striving to fit in. I often sat in the back of the classroom, where my grade ranking determined where I was to sit. When the French teacher tested us, by pointing at a student, I hoped I wouldn't be picked.

At dinner in Teri Mangal, the mujahedeen kept asking me if I was strong enough. We would be climbing 7,000 feet up to peaks as high as 16,000 feet. I had climbed Wyoming's Wind River Valley, 13,000 feet mountains, carrying a 30- pound pack. But I had my doubts. I wasn't fit, and my extra weight would definitely slow me down. The lack of oxygen at those heights was a factor, but I was tough and persistent. I might not be naturally strong, but I made up for it with endurance, grit, and a "failure-is-not-an-option" attitude.

In the evening, the mosquitoes stung, and welts grew on my arms and legs. The French woman doctor gave me a can of flea powder for the night. I felt we were on the threshold of existence, all creature comforts left behind.

On the Afghan border, lying on a cot set up by the French doctors, John said regretfully, "I missed my wedding. It was meant to be today." I had forgotten about John's wedding plans with Rose back in England. It seemed like a different reality, fancy dresses, churches with steeples, wedding cakes. Nearly two months had passed, and we were still at the beginning of the journey, in the hands of the Afghan freedom fighters. I suddenly remembered my New York City artist and filmmaker friend, Sarah. She had shown me a photo of herself standing on Wall Street with a sign around her neck that said, "Siberia or Bust," to raise money for her trip to the Soviet Union. My motto was "Panjshir Valley or Bust."

In the late afternoon, our caravan of over fifty men, led by Commander Shaskti, began to climb the mountain—a straight-up dirt path edged with dwarf evergreens. Several other commanders were traveling under Shaskti's leadership. Stocky workhorses and mules carried the ammunition boxes strapped with ropes and hung like two full fishing nets on both sides of the animals' bellies. Several horses and their guides were designated to be up front and on the lookout for mines. Thirty or more feet behind the horses, John and Commander Shaskti, a former policeman with stubble instead of a beard, led the caravan. Shaskti was transporting arms from China. The Chinese characters stamped on the outside of the metal boxes gave away their origin. China had not declared its official allegiance at this time, but there was no doubt what side they took in this war. The ammunition would have to last into the spring in this northern region.

Once the snow started, the mountain passes would be impassable. John and I were hitching a ride with this caravan and were not informed about the exact military drop-off location. The Jamiat leaders in Pakistan had promised us that someone would bring us to Istalif and then to the Panjshir Valley. We had to trust them.

Shaskti's macho men followed with more horses heavily loaded with ammunition. I walked in the back, behind all the packhorses. Two young Afghans stayed close to me, one tall and one short.

After a few hours of a steep, unrelenting hike, the sun set quickly behind the scraggly snow-covered mountain tops. In the distance, yellow lights flashed across the black horizon. Bombs were attacking Georgi, the Afghani Soviet-backed government post. We took a circuitous route, a safer alternative path around the siege, where I was told the mujahedeen were winning. I wondered if the more direct way would have been an easier climb.

I wore Timberland hiking boots and kept a good pace, as we climbed higher and higher. Some of the men wore flip-flops; others wore badly fitted military boots that produced terrible blisters. There were some young teens walking barefoot on their tough calluses. John was ahead, but I was not sure how far away. I started counting the trees on my left. I counted to ten and then started over. The counting focused my mind, made me forget how tired I was, and marked the distance in manageable increments.

Hiking into the late evening, a cold chill set in the high altitude air. Two companions and I took a short rest under a broad ash tree. A short break to catch our breath. No prayers. No tea. When I stood up, one of the men took my backpack and its heavy contents—the camera, film, sleeping bag, Walkman, and shortwave radio. Lighter now, I would not fall far behind the caravan.

As dark night clouds covered the stars and moon, we caught up with the long chain of horses. I heard only the sound of their hooves. All the neighing, snorting, and whinnying had stopped. These horses' ancestors had carried silk, spices, gems, and gold on this same road through the Khyber pass, over one peak, down a ridge. Mountain passages traversed for centuries. I felt a strange confidence in the simplicity of this journey. Walking with these men, I was part of a long lineage of travelers.

Off in the distance, white flashes of light silhouetted our figures against the dark background. Strange rumbling sounded in the distance. It could be thunder or bombs. By now, we had put some distance between us and the closest government post. The government posts were controlled by Soviet-backed, Afghan militias. Unless there was a planned attack, the mujahedeen usually kept their distance. If these were battle sounds, the only possible military position would be the government post. I had no way to find out what was really going on. My two young companions didn't speak much English. Exhaustion filled my body, turning into heaviness in my chest. I placed one foot in front of the other. Cold seeped in through my skin and settled in my bones. The light cotton tunic was damp and the only warmth came from the wool patu blanket wrapped around me. It was freezing. A wind howled through the mountains. I was shivering and walking, one foot in front of the other. I could manage a one-two count, over and over, steadying myself through the repetition. My chest ached and burned from the constant deep breaths and lack of oxygen.

Up the next mountain, I dropped far behind the horses. The two men stayed behind with me. I was going forward by momentum alone. The faraway flashes of lightning now surrounded me, blinded me. The explosive thunder frightened me. I grabbed the back of the taller man's tunic to keep on the path. I couldn't see anything. One foot in front of the other. One, two, one, two, one, two. Rain pelted down, icy rain, slippery rain. I moved forward. Flash. Blindness. Darkness.

Invisible hands grabbed me, shoved me, and pushed me onto the back of a big horse. I held its rough mane for balance. I had lost all orientation. The horse's wet fur and wool blanket saddle gave off a musty barn animal smell. A barn would have been a palace to me now. Any shelter would do. The rain, my drenched clothes, and my wet skin made a pool of water on the back of the enormous horse. I hung on to the mane and tried not to fall off. The rain shot down hard, cold, penetrating.

After a few more hours, we stopped in front of a mud building. The drenched caravan horses were tied to trees. Fifty men crammed into one room. There was no room to stretch out so I sat on the floor, held my knees curled up in front and waited. A puddle formed around my spot on the dirt floor. There was no tea, nothing at all to warm us, just shelter from the rain. We waited until the rain stopped. I looked around for John, but couldn't find him. My brain was so numb, I didn't dwell on where he could be.

Back on my feet, I started again on the journey towards Istalif, walking. The horse had disappeared as magically as had it appeared. The sun rose, and I could see the rocky path. The men did not pray, conserving all their energy for the next mountain climb. The path narrowed and narrowed until only one person or horse could pass at a time. Single file, we carried forward for hours. It had been a night and a day since we had left Teri Mangal, and we were going into a second night.

On one side of the path, there was a steep drop into a canyon so I pressed my right shoulder against the rock on the other side to feel safe. One false step and a horse could tumble over the edge. There was no room for error here. Alexander the Great had climbed these insurmountable mountains. Nomads had been here before. Men, women, and children had traveled through here. And so would I.

However, modern guerrilla warfare was reduced to basic resources here. There were no tanks, helicopters, not even military uniforms. Horses carried military arms, and they were pushed to their limits. Even I was reduced to juvenile tactics to survive. I asked one of my companions, who had been by my side since we started, "When will we get there?" using sign language.

"Soon," he shouted back, a few steps ahead of me, "Near." His few words of English reassured me. This question and answer routine kept me going, around one bend, then another. We didn't stop. The same cliff pressed against my right shoulder throughout the journey.

"No, you're wrong," the game no longer sustained me.

"Soon," the other shorter companion pushed me from behind.

"You said it was near," I whispered.

Trancelike, I fought to stay upright. Jelly-muscled, I staggered now. I was past the zone, past all physical endurance, past all constructive thoughts. My first reassuring thought was that death was an option. I should lie here and die. This was the time and place for me to die. It didn't seem like a dramatic thought, just the solution. I needed to die in Afghanistan. Right here. Death would release me.

"I stop here," I said and felt I had completely surrendered to the situation. Whatever happened, happened. I would stay behind, lay down, and die. I had completely accepted this decision not to exist, to fully let go. I had no fight or struggle with death. I was in a welcoming, peaceful, and conscious space.

Both companions, one on each side, shoved me forward, one short thrust at a time. Then we stopped. It was not me who stopped but some rag doll carried by these two men. When I was ready to die, help came. These men were like angels who felt they had a duty and obligation to save me. I had let go, accepted my fate. I didn't believe it was anyone's obligation to save me. It could not have been easy to take care of someone unprepared to endure this march. But they did.

This physical endurance test brought me close to death and to a profound realization that I could be comfortable with it. I didn't have to fear death when it would come. The ultimate rest would find me, when the time was right. I would pursue life at its fullest, without any existential angst about death.

On my second night inside Afghanistan, we stopped at a thatched roof tea house high in the Himalayas. I felt alone, although I was surrounded by the mujahedeen. It was an independent and strong emotional state, one that made me feel uniquely confident in myself and able to nourish myself from the power I found within. We were served hot green tea poured over white sugar crystals and dry sweet biscuits. Then, I slept for hours.

It was late morning when I woke. I couldn't move. All my muscles were stiff, unbending. I couldn't even stand up to go to the outhouse. I didn't want anyone to know that I was frozen in this spot like a rock. The Wyoming Mountains were hills compared to this terrain. The pace had been beyond my limit. I had no idea how I could go forward in this body, which was fused to this spot. Slowly, like oil squirted into the Tin Man's joints, my body began to bend. I could stand, but I wobbled, unsure that this body could carry me up another mountain.

John was not with us, and I had no idea how he was faring. Later, I learned that he had been lost with a small group of mujahedeen. He was not there for me to rely on, and my guardian angels did not have the strength to pull me through another day of hiking.

I stepped outside. The tall companion motioned me over to a grey horse. This grey speckled horse was for me. He introduced me to the horse's handler, who would guide me to Istalif. I couldn't have afforded the horse or the guide on our limited budget. (Renting a horse was out of the question. During wartime, the owner would have no assurance that the horse would be returned.) It was the mujahedeen who gave me the horse to carry me to Istalif, and I was grateful.

Riding on the steady horse, I could relax on the winding trails through the villages. The birds flew south in V formations in the vast, cloudless sky. Our caravan crossed gushing rivers without incident. My guide was skilled with the horse I rode. I felt transported to a simpler time, when most villagers farmed and raised animals and the seasons marked time. But we couldn't stop. Far off in the distance, I could see the tall walls that surrounded family compounds. These villages belonged to the Hezbi Islami group, archrivals with Massoud's Northern Alliance. Each village had an alliance with a particular mujahedeen group, and hospitality was extended or requested based on these relationships. The Pashtu tribal group I had traveled with in Kandahar last year would not be open or congenial to the Tajik Jamiat group now hosting me. These tribal lines ran deep. These conflicts had existed for centuries.

The horse's side-to-side rocking comforted me. My body recovered on the back of the beast. The aches and stiffness began to feel more like what you feel a day after a good workout. I sensed something sticky between my legs. It couldn't be! I was hoping I would not get my period on the trip. I was taking birth control pills every other day to stretch my last 28-day supply. There were no tampons or sanitary pads available anywhere in the vicinity. There were no bathrooms, showers, or any proper way to clean myself.

I was not sure what was going on down there. Under the patu blanket, I reached into my pants and touched myself. My fingers were all bloody. Terrible timing! These men would be reminded I was a woman, like their women, wives, sisters, daughters, mothers, aunts, all hidden behind family compound walls. They were deemed dirty, not deserving of the male privileges of freedom and choice because of their biological function. The third-sex, Western woman spell would be broken if the mujahedeen saw me menstruate.

I reached for the roll of toilet paper in my backpack, and using the patu blanket that covered my waist and thighs as camouflage, I stuffed the wads of paper between my legs as a temporary measure. Another hour passed on horseback; I was lulled and rested by the ride. A refreshing breeze clipped my bangs, and my eyelids jolted open after a minute's nap.

Ahmed, the commander of our breakaway group of about twenty men, stopped in front of a small whitewashed mosque situated on a hill by a stream. He shouted at the men, tied my horse to a nearby tree, then changed his mind and had my guide put me further away from the mosque, near the stream. I slid off the horse. The guide gave me a long lingering look. I began to suspect that the commander saw the blood and wanted me far from the others.

I was covered in blood, soaked through my garment, the horse's blanket stained brown-red. Thankfully, the patu draped over my front and back hid most of the mess. There was a small waterfall near the stream. I asked my guide to take me to a secluded spot behind a tree and near the waterfall. He stood by the tree with his back to me. I stepped under the waterfall, fully clothed. The icy mountain water hit me, washed over me, stripped away layers of caked-on blood, dirt, and sweat, rinsing over and over me like a baptism. The men prayed together in the mosque. My spirituality was more private and individual in its pursuit. I didn't have a community like they did.

A campfire was lit outside. I washed myself and felt purified. I decided it would be OK to be among these men again and restored myself. I had been gone a long time. When I returned it was dark. A flat-shaped moon hung over the mosque. Ahmed shouted in broken English, "Where you go? What you doing?"

"I was washing in the river," I said, rubbing my hands together, miming my words to explain. "Everything is OK." I walked to the fire to dry myself. Standing in front of the fire, my teeth chattered and I shivered. Ahmed watched me intently, with a sneer on his face. He seemed disgusted by the sight of me.

I picked up my backpack, which the guide had left by my feet, and entered the dark mosque. Ahmed marched behind me in loud stomps. I pulled out my shortwave radio and offered it to him, expecting him to be delighted with the treat. The mujahedeen enjoyed listening to the BBC world news, local music, and commentaries.

"Holy place. No radio in mosque," he said, handing the offending equipment back to me.

Tears welled up in my eyes. I didn't want him to see me crying. Life was hard—the physical endurance, lack of food, menstruation, and now the admonishment. I found a corner far from the mosque door and the rest of the mujahedeen and rolled out my sleeping bag on the stone floor. I was still damp, cold, and slipped into the warm down cocoon. I pulled the patu blanket over my head.

"You leave," Ahmed tugged at my sleeping bag.

"You want me to sleep outside?" I said in disbelief. I didn't think I would be safe outside by myself. I was being unfairly treated like an outcast. I hadn't done anything wrong. A woman's cycle is the most natural biological necessity. My menstruation was what made me a woman; it was my fertility, a core aspect of my strength. Women have been shamed by their periods, their femininity, for centuries.

I didn't budge. Ahmed would have to physically pick me up and throw me out of the mosque. The part of me that was strong came alive.

"Forget about him. You stay here," the second commander said, and stepped between Ahmed and myself. He was tall, broad-shouldered, muscular, and spoke excellent English.

This was the first time Baba Fawad spoke to me. His rich baritone voice was deep and friendly. Prince-like, he had shown up at the exact moment necessary to avoid a major confrontation between Ahmed and me. I was thankful for his commanding ways. Ahmed backed down and let me stay. In minutes, I fell asleep on the floor of a mosque, next to a band of twenty men.

CHAPTER 5

THE LION OF PANJSHIR

When I woke up the next morning, Baba Fawad stood near me like a bodyguard, staring at me with a soul-penetrating gaze. During the night, my clothes had dried off from my body heat. And my period had stopped as suddenly as it had appeared. These tough conditions, the birth control pills, and lack of food had made my period irregular, shortening its duration to a few hours of heavy flow.

Fawad followed me as I went outside and helped me to mount the grey horse. He had replaced yesterday's guide and walked next to me, while I rode on the horse. He spoke about Istalif, as only a native of the place could, describing in vivid detail the snow-peaked mountains surrounding his village, his beautiful home. I could picture the turquoise and green pottery fired in wood burning kilns, the blue lapis lazuli jewelry available in the market. His English was the best of all the mujahedeen. He had been shy about meeting me at first, but now he didn't leave my side.

"You will see most special town," he said. "No war there, everyone happy."

All I could think about was food. My hunger had become a chronic condition. The infrequent, short tea breaks relieved briefly my parched mouth. The caravan carried no food provisions, just military supplies. Back in Pakistan, John had loved to tease me about my short temper when my blood sugar dropped. He had still not shown up. It had been four days since I last saw him. I hoped he was OK. We needed each other to fulfill the BBC and CBS contracts. The pace had become easier, but everyone was worn out. The horses were dragging, too. Some of the men who wore the army boots were limping; they had terrible blisters. At the next rest stop, we sat on a bunch of boulders under a canopy of trees. The youngest mujahedeen, a 16 year-old-boy, lean, with no facial hair, pulled off his boots. He hadn't been wearing any socks, and his blisters were broken, oozing, and bleeding. I pulled a patch of moleskin and nail scissors out of my backpack, then cut a square of moleskin, folded it in two, cut a half circle, and made a bandage to patch his wounds. When I turned around, an older mujahedeen in his twenties with a similar wound, pointed at his blistered feet. I repeated the treatment. After I finished that man, another requested help, then another. My meager supplies were accepted as gifts from Allah. All praise to Allah, the men said, looking up at the sky. I took no credit for my simple first-aid skills. Islam taught that all blessings came from Allah. And I agreed that everything came from a higher source.

We started to bond, the mujahedeen and me. We were in this together, traveling to Istalif, where food, warmth, and rest were promised. We were banded together by basic human needs, and in a few hours, we would take care of them.

High up on the back of the horse, I could peer over the walls that lined both sides of the road. I could see the bountiful vineyards on the outskirts of Istalif on the Shomali Plain. Ripe grapes hung on the vines. Baba Fawad brought me a cluster of green grapes. I leaned over the horse, as he popped one green grape into my mouth. It burst open, and sweet juice trickled out of the punctured fruit's flesh. I swished the ball in my mouth, slowly chewing the satisfying and delicious mass.

We left behind the lush orchards and entered Istalif's busy bazaar. Men of all ages ambled by, dressed in fresh clothes, topped by turbans wrapped around their heads. Small birds chirped in wood-and-wire cages hung in the doorway of an open stall. I saw turquoise and green pottery, displayed on wooden tables outside an open air workshop. Bulls pulled carts piled high with full sacks of flour, potatoes, and other foods. Simple geometric wool rugs lay on the dirt ground for passersby to admire and, hopefully, buy. The snow-covered, majestic mountains glistened in the background.

Smiling people with no cares surrounded us—twenty mujahedeen carrying their weapons on their backs and I, an American filmmaker with her camera—as we waded through the market, an incongruous and disturbing scene. The horses and the rest of the caravan moved on to their final destination. I never found out where they hid their military arms for the winter.

I was living outside of everyday reality, yet I felt completely absorbed in the moment. Travel brought me out of my daily habits where life was more predictable. Here, all possibilities existed and could awaken new states of awareness. On the hill overlooking the town, the Afghan government post protected Istalif by keeping the Hezbi Islami and Jamiat factions from fighting each other, by diverting the Soviets with false information, and, generally, by staying out of the war as much as possible. Fawad bought me a Fanta orange soda from one of the market stalls and went on to explain the local politics. The bubbly drink tasted saccharin-sweet, unnatural, out of place in this old world market.

Fawad took me to the house of a wealthy man who lived near the market and arranged for us to stay there. Our rich host, Fawad, and I sat on elegant rugs over a wooden floor. A young servant boy served us rice, lamb stew, yogurt, and naan bread. We drank cup after cup of sugared green tea, mostly in silence. I felt full for the first time since leaving Pakistan. The servant took me to a private room with a raised bed, where I slept in comfort.

The next morning, John finally showed up at my host's house in great spirits. John's Afghan guides had asked the merchants in the bazaar where I was staying. The latest news was easy to get in the market. John joked about how he prayed for grapes and Allah delivered. He said the mujahedeen loved his story about his wishing for grapes and Allah providing. Since it was grape season, we were indulging in grapes of all varieties.

"What happened to you?" I asked.

"The first night, in the middle of the thunderstorm, a small group of us separated from the caravan. We were lost."

"Were you OK?"

He smiled. Whatever difficulties he had faced were behind him and not BBC newsworthy.

Later, in tourist mode, we took time to stop and see new sites. Fawad was our guide. First, the rug makers showed us their simple wooden looms on the dirt floors where they worked. Then, we went to the tanning factory, where they made sheepskin vests. The smell, a mixture of ammonia and skunk roadkill, was from sheep hides hanging to dry after they had been dipped in a salt acid solution. Fawad surprised me with an embroidered sheepskin vest, which he gave me to keep me warm. Its strong smell could not compete with my five-day unwashed body odor.

Elaborate schemes were devised to keep us safe; we moved each night from house to house. We were guests of merchants, farmers, and Afghan mullahs, all leaders in the community. Fawad didn't want to cause them any problems with the Afghan government post so we plotted our moves carefully. When we left one house, we took circuitous routes to the new one. Loud "As-Salaam-Alaikum" were spoken all around to welcome us. I was sure the whole village knew where we were staying.

The Commander at the Afghan government post sent a message: "There are journalists in Istalif." He wanted ten mujahedeen and four goats in exchange for not alerting the Russians. Commander Shaksti sent word back: "No journalists here." Shaksti took over our escape and moved us clandestinely out of town, to a nearby village. Later, John and I were informed that one of the homes where we stayed was bombed.

The death and damage to our host's home made me angry at myself and our guides, who had traipsed us through this idyllic town. I was much more aware of what it meant to be a war journalist now. Anyone participating in a war was drawn into the horror and could be responsible for more destruction and pain. It didn't matter whether I came for a peace story or an ambush, I was involved. Retaliation was inevitable, and I felt responsible for what happened.

At the mud house outside of Istalif, there was a loud knock on the door. John and I were on the alert, but it was just a guide, coming to take us further up the mountain into a more remote place.

Fawad was now in charge of our small group of four. Shaksti bid us goodbye. John pushed Fawad to take us to Massoud, but we had little say over our schedule or routes and were rarely told when or where we were going next.

"Farda," tomorrow, Fawad said in Dari.

Always tomorrow!

"Is John your husband?" Fawad asked.

"No," I said. "Are you married?"

"Yes, I have four wives."

"Where do they live?"

"Here, in Istalif."

"Any children?"

"Yes, three. One's a baby, a two-year old, and a three-year old."

It was hard to imagine the life of the women who shared this husband. I wanted a man who only wanted me. However, Fawad carried himself with a sexual power that I had not noticed before, and this moved something in me. I walked close to him, bumping into him on purpose, teasing him. He walked straight, ignored my silly gestures, and strode to our next destination.

We arrived at a two-story mountain house built out of wood, high above a raging river in a gorge. Millions of stars shone bright and seemed close enough to touch. It was cold outside. A small, cast iron stove in the corner of the room radiated heat. The food was plentiful. I slept under five heavy floral blanket-like mattresses, piled one on top of the other, to insulate me from the mountain chill. The weight was stifling and uncomfortable. I unrolled my down sleeping bag next to Baba Fawad and climbed in.

When the men started to snore and heavy breathing filled the room, I pushed myself closer to Baba Fawad. I felt his heat, his pulse, his breath near me. I hid my hands under the patu and inched closer to him, so I could touch his hand. We secretly intertwined fingers; his knuckles fascinated me. He dropped my hand and left the room, stepping outside on the balcony overlooking the rapid stream below.

I followed him. The cold wind slapped my face. The stars reached far into other galaxies. Our breaths steamed in the winter darkness. He pulled me close. I felt his hardness under his pants. He lifted me up, and I wrapped my legs around his waist. I felt weightless in his arms. He leaned against the house. The river rippled through me, gushing through my veins, shooting his energy through me.

We leaned back against the house wall, steamy under the patu blanket he wrapped around us. I touched a large scar on his muscular chest.

"What happened?"

"I was shot by the mujahedeen."

"But you're a mujahedeen. How could that happen?"

"I was an Afghan soldier before."

"What?" I asked.

"I wanted to fight the Russians, when they invaded."

The intimacy we shared and this unfolding story of how he was shot by his own people, connected me to him. This was not the way George had entered my heart and nurtured me. Baba Fawad's maleness, his power, his intensity, his history evoked a warrior prowess that I wanted. I thought, if I had four husbands, I would have a strong, courageous one like Baba Fawad; a gentle, caring, loving one like George; an intellectual Dr. Zhivago type; and, lastly, an artist type. I could get into this four-to-one ratio, as long as the tables were turned.

Fawad explained how he went to the government post to join the fight, thinking they were against the Soviets. Factual information was hard to come by. Communications were sporadic. Everything came through word of mouth. Anyone could easily be misled. Commanders, mujahedeen, journalists, and villagers were often in the dark about what was happening. Without a wireless radio or newspapers, villagers had to figure things out the hard way. The post commander didn't care that Fawad was totally confused about who was fighting whom.

Once he signed up in the Afghan army, they gave Fawad his uniform, trained him, and gave him a gun to shoot his fellow Afghan countrymen. After he realized his terrible mistake, the mujahedeen ambushed his army camp and shot him.

"This bullet came from mujahedeen," Fawad told me, "I wanted to be mujahedeen commander. I must escape Afghan army."

At the hospital, a doctor removed the bullet that had ripped through Fawad's chest, bypassing major organs. The massive scar was a reminder of who he was really fighting. Then, he defected and joined the Northern Alliance Group, closely tied into the Jamiat Group. If the Afghan army had caught him, he would have been killed as a traitor.

Many other Afghans stayed in the army, held government positions, and generally helped the mujahedeen from the inside as informers. The motto, "You can only rent an Afghan, never own one," was demonstrated over and over.

Listening to Baba Fawad's voice on this night high up in the mountains aroused my passions. I felt an attachment to him and his people. Fawad talked of better days in Istalif, when it was a major tourist site in the 70s. The ancient canals and fertile lands made this region the breadbasket of Afghanistan. Hippies visited on their way overland to India and told their friends about the amazing generosity of the Afghans. They picnicked in places like this wooden mountain house with the stone terrace. Fawad had met many foreigners and learned English from them in tea shops. He had an affair with a Swedish woman. He was so attractive; he probably had many other affairs with English-speaking women, too.

I told him stories about my first trip into Afghanistan and Kandahar, my own life back home in America, and going to film school in England. I even mentioned my fiancé, George. He listened and didn't ask many questions.

He gathered some twigs, took the kitchen's firewood, and built a fire on the terrace's makeshift hearth. The wood and fire sparked and sputtered. Then, he brought out the blackened kettle to boil water and made us tea on the open fire. We stayed warm sitting close together through the night. The spark of love darted inside me, so unexpected, but so deep under my skin. This man connected to a part of me that sparkled, felt alive, driven.

In the morning, I was high from the connection of the night before. Our small troop marched out in the open through the Istalif market, where there were now over a thousand merchants. There were only four of us, Fawad, the Afghan guide, John, and myself, as well as a donkey to carry our gear and provisions. John was relaxed now that we were heading toward our destination. He pulled out a cigarette, handed one to Fawad, and then lit the cigarette with his silver lighter. They both started to smoke.

"What kind of military strategist do you think Massoud is?" John asked Fawad, speculating about the charismatic leader.

"He's brilliant," answered Fawad, full of reverence for his leader. "He makes Soviets afraid, they can't win against him, too strong, too smart—best warrior for Afghanistan. Everyone love him."

In the evening, we stumbled onto a Bedouin camp from the Kyrgyz tribe. Their pelt-covered yurts flapped in the winds. Drumbeats and wail-like singing grew louder, as we found ourselves in the middle of a wedding. Instantly, we were invited to be guests of honor. We sat next to the musicians tapping a large round drum, as steamy trays of roasted lamb and rice were placed in front of us. A beer yogurt fermented drink followed, the first alcoholic beverage I had seen since arriving in Afghanistan. Fawad and our guide refused politely. Islamic law, they told us. But the wedding party was not Muslim. They had their own customs so women and men mixed more freely, due to their nomadic life high in the mountains. The bride wore rich, red thick robes and silk embroidery, with small gold coins sewn into her wedding costume. The coins tinkled when she moved and danced. Her head was uncovered and her round, deeply tanned face shone in the firelight. After a week on this trip, this wedding feast looked like it could be fun, but John was eager to press on. After our dinner with the Bedouins, I grabbed Fawad's arm and we headed back in the dark.

We were avoiding certain villages that might inform on us. However, the donkey hee-hawed so loudly that dogs barked and people came out to see what all the ruckus was about. So, we sent the donkey back with our guide. We walked hand in hand, Baba Fawad and I, fresh lovers, with nothing to hide in the shadows of the night. The wedding alcohol had warmed me, and I floated in our romance.

John dreamt of recipes and menus from his favorite restaurants back in London. He recited the ingredients and cooking instructions for each dish in his own rap-like poetry: "Pound chicken breasts. Place cheese and ham on each breast. Fold chicken over cheese and ham. Secure with toothpicks. Mix flour and paprika. Coat chicken pieces. Fry, baby, fry."

* * *

After a long rest in an abandoned shelter for animals, our guide, having returned the donkey, caught up with us. He rode on one horse and a second horse trailed behind him by a lead rope.

John was getting more and more irritable. His exhaustion and frustration with how long it was taking to get to the Panjshir Valley were compounding. And he was disgruntled with his horse. He didn't like horses or animals in general. When he mounted his brown horse, the horse's muscles tightened and refused to budge, and its head hung forward. The guide held the rein and coaxed the horse with sweet clicking sounds. They moved forward together, but not at a steady pace, rather more like the guide pulling the horse. John cursed his horse, when he stalled and would not move, but it didn't help, and the horse kept acting like a belligerent toddler.

I was delighted with my mahogany brown horse and rode him on the open plains and ancient dry river beds. The next mountain pass was in the distance, and my horse galloped, my hair flying wild, blowing through the wind. I felt a sense of serenity, a sense of existing beyond the boundaries of my ego, a sense of timelessness. Hours passed by in minutes, I was so thoroughly focused on the present.

We stopped at a shady walnut grove for tea and hot food. Elegant old men with white turbans and tunics wore hand-embroidered vests in gemstone colors. They watched us, as we enjoyed our lunch. The children in miniature tunics, dirty from playing hard, snuck up close to check me out. My light brown hair, streaked blonde from the sun, caught their attention and they giggled. They hadn't seen many light-haired people. Fawad handed out hard candies, and the kids unwrapped the sweets immediately and popped them in their mouths. Big grins appeared.

John, still stuck in his bad mood, was fuming at his horse. He suddenly got up and slugged the horse's face with his fist. I was in shock. Who does that? And to an innocent animal, tied to a tree with a feedbag hanging around its neck! The horse waited until John walked past his back leg, then kicked him to the ground.

"It serves you right," I shouted at him.

John's meanness could have been a disaster. We were nowhere near proper medical facilities.

"Are you crazy?" I said.

Fortunately, he was only bruised; I suspect more in ego than in body.

* * *

We continued trekking through lush green fields with purple grapes dangling from the vines. Sweet, juicy grapes: tangy, citrusy, like fine wine; we ate them harvested from this land. The flavors captured the vast plains. John walked with Fawad and seemed visibly thrilled that we would be arriving in the Panjshir Valley soon. Our guide and I rode together. The two beasts carried us through the Salang Pass, where emeralds, rubies, and lapis lazuli were buried in rocks. We didn't suffer any of the hardships from the first days through the Hindu Kush. And our destination was around the corner.

Up until now, the cease-fire was just a rumor. Nothing could be taken as factual, until we saw it for ourselves. The horses brought us to a wide dirt road at the mouth of the Panjshir Valley. On the side of the road, Afghan soldiers sat on the back of a truck out in the open. Mujahedeen walked with their Kalashnikovs hanging across their chests. Blond Russians hung out smoking in front of the government post, once the Afghan's King's summer palace. So it was true! Massoud had negotiated a cease-fire with the Soviet-backed Panjshir commander. Nowhere else could the Soviet soldiers relax out in the open. They were easy targets for the mujahedeen snipers.

The mud and wood-beamed homes of the village were built on steep slopes. The river gushed below. Kids ran up and down the hills for fun. Fawad led John and me into a beautiful home, where there was a large open room decorated with many large tribal rugs. In the back, there was a garden full of fig and apple trees, and a gurgling stream ran through it. The host, a former cook for American and British dignitaries before the war, served us omelets and French fries. I almost expected ketchup. We enjoyed the hospitality and the Western food.

Now that we were staying in Commander Massoud's village, Fawad had started to put some distance between us. Our unguarded affection on the hike was over. That night, I was not sure if it was the food or the water, but I had constant diarrhea. Rushing out into the garden in the dark, squatting behind a fruit tree, I could not find the outhouse and was too embarrassed to wake anyone. The urgent compelling explosions kept me up all night. I listened to Lou Reed's "Walk on the Wild Side" on my Walkman, which reminded me of the fun riding next to Fawad, while trying to distract myself from the acute stomach ache.

The next morning, John and I made a plan to interview Commander Massoud, and Fawad confirmed our appointment. John would ask the questions. I would translate for them. We had heard rumors that Massoud distrusted journalists. Maybe the roundabout journey through Istalif was his way to test whether we were serious about meeting him. There was a divide between the freelance journalists like us and the on-staff reporters who would fly into Kabul and get the government propaganda story. They were in and out in the same day, or they stayed in no-man's land for a few hours to interview an official representative and then taxied back to Peshawar, boasting about going "inside."

John and I were the hard core types. We did whatever it took to find out what was really going on, to get the real story. We traveled with the mujahedeen, ate their food, and drank tea side by side with them. We made our own contacts, developed relationships, and saw much more than staff reporters. Many times, our stories were initiated by our experiences and what we felt mattered and, less often, from reactions to the current events of the moment.

Fawad took us up a steep climb to a patio outside a mud house where Commander Massoud was conducting business. He was a skinny man with sharply sculpted facial features, deep-set eyes—

dark, black, piercing—and a short goatee. His right shoulder jutted out, as if dislocated, and twitched spasmodically, a reflex setting it back in place every ten minutes or so. It looked painful. Now, I saw what Ed Girardet meant about the twitch.

Under the grapevine trellis, I set up the tripod and camera. I translated John's questions into French and Massoud's answers back into English, while I filmed with our Super 8 camera. My concentration was fully on the job at hand. I was aware that the sound would not be great. I was using the built-in mic attached to the body of the camera, and the camera motor was loud, which would be a liability in the editing room.

Massoud was gracious, comfortable in front of the camera. The story poured out of him like a ballad. In the spring of 1983, his men had fought hard. Their land had protected them—the steep inclines, the river, a canyon to trap invaders. The women, children, and old people hid in the caves of the nearby mountains. Then the ammunition ran out. This was the seventh siege they had endured. Surely, this time, they would lose, would have to surrender. Defeat seemed inevitable.

"I sent a young man to surrender," Massoud told us. "We had no more food."

But his men would not give up. They kept fighting, and then the Soviets stopped fighting back. They didn't know what was happening. This was odd. Then the message came from the commander at the government post that the Soviets wanted a cease-fire, even though they were still invading the rest of the country. The tactic was brilliant for both sides. They would co-exist. This was a symbol of what could be possible, an example of peace, and a truce that could spread to the rest of Afghanistan.

"I'm fighting for a free world, not only a free Afghanistan," Massoud told us. He hated the totalitarianism of the Soviet Union and the extreme Islamic fundamentalism of some Afghani groups. He prayed daily and contemplated the Koran's spiritual message. And he refused to be intimidated by murderous forms of Islam. Massoud practiced a moderate type of Sunni Islam, with strong Sufi overtones. He read texts written by the Islamic mystic al-Ghazali nightly. He quoted from the Sufi Master's book, which he carried with him everywhere, even into battle:

This, the whole science of self-discipline and holy war: to purify one's heart of all hatred towards one's fellow creatures, of all lust for the world, and of all preoccupation with sensual things; such is the path of the Sufis.

Massoud poured us tea, his hand steady. It was a humble gesture to serve us. The Afghan custom to honor us as guests felt magnified coming from Commander Massoud. John and I knew we were in the presence of an extraordinary man. He was a spiritual leader seeking a path for eventual peace, as well as a strategic and powerful military ruler.

In the afternoon, we followed Massoud in his daily life, listening to the mullahs, the elders of the tribe, holding counsel on governing this Tajik tribal region in the ancient ways. Fawad would translate key points. Young Afghani runners approached Massoud to sign commands, orders for goods, petitions. Massoud, a busy man, governed this small state, an island of peace surrounded by war.

In the evening, Massoud was the guest of honor at a buzkashi sports event, where horses that were bred and trained to charge each other did so. To win, the riders grabbed a bloated, dead calf from each other and deposited the carcass in a circle drawn on the ground. Each man for himself, the horses circled, stampeded, charged at each other. The earth shook, red dust clouds covered the whole spectacle. The villagers shouted and howled at each player's courage and prowess when he stole the beast from his opponent. Massoud stood among his people, a part of the crowd, but also apart.

After the Soviet invasion, Massoud, who was an engineering student, and his father, a police officer, had aspired for Massoud to be a military leader. His tactics, the trust he inspired, and his organizational skills were formidable. The U.S. never supplied him with the arms that his nemesis, Gulbuddin Hekmatyar, leader of the Hezbi Islami group, managed to gain. It was, possibly, a fatal mistake for the U.S. to not supply Massoud with arms. Hekmatyar was hated by most ordinary Afghans for ruthlessly eliminating anyone who opposed him, especially Afghans from competing tribes. He commanded from the safety of Peshawar, with no qualms about attacking rival mujahedeen groups when it benefited his cause. Some experts claimed Hekmatyar was supported by the Americans so that the Soviets would have their own Vietnam war—no side winning, just constant killings and draining of resources. Some say the U.S. backed Hekmatyar because he spoke English and Massoud didn't. Later on, Massoud fought the Taliban, who had yet to emerge on the scene. Massoud thought their religious ideology was too restrictive, especially concerning women's rights to education. He also opposed their fundamentalist Arab backing, later led by Osama bin Laden. This strong stand against the Taliban led to Massoud's martyrdom. Two fake journalists, suicide Taliban jihadists from Saudi Arabia, hid an explosive in their camera when they interviewed Massoud two days before 9/11. They blew up Massoud, his advisors, themselves, and everyone in the vicinity. Ahmad Shah Massoud was a hero and became a martyr.

Many Afghans had hoped that Massoud would unite Afghanistan into a peaceful nation. This dream ended when Massoud was murdered and the U.S. invaded Afghanistan. The Taliban became as strong as ever. Afghan factions, who hated the Soviets previously, now hated the Americans, uniting against anyone who opposed the Taliban, including the United States. Billions of dollars of U.S. taxpayer money meant for rebuilding the country ended up in a few greedy pockets, enabling drug lords, selfish opportunists, insensitive soldiers, and arrogant mercenaries to undermine any progress for the country's recovery. War perpetuated crimes and further suffering.

John and I stayed for a few more days after the interview with Massoud. I made a list of shots I had so far: the bazaar open as usual, the terraced farms, the land plowed, the homes built into the sides of the canyon, the government post unguarded, the mujahedeen's training camp, Massoud's interview, the buzkashi game—all great visuals for the cease-fire story. I was in the flow, enjoying the process of creation, satisfied with the work completed.

* * *

A long line of women and children were standing outside a makeshift clinic near the bazaar, where the four French doctors we had met at Teri Mangal were working. They had no proper sanitation, no running water, and few medical supplies. They greeted us with enthusiasm, an instant camaraderie of shared experiences like a team reunited after a victory game. When we arrived inside the busy waiting room, a young boy was removing a large scorpion, placing it in a glass jar and carrying it outside. Massoud had made it possible for women doctors to work here, his French whores, as some rival mujahedeen groups called them. Conservative mullahs did not allow male doctors to treat women. In a refugee camp, a Pakistani male doctor was stoned to death after treating a woman alone in her tent. Sick women walked for miles to see the French woman doctor, their only chance for medical care.

I spotted the French woman doctor, who had praised my French language skills. She looked tired and gaunt. She told me how, before they made it to the Panjshir Valley, they operated on a young man who had been injured by a mine. He had screamed and screamed from the pain of the surgery; they didn't have any anesthesia. They left him to recover in the tent. A few hours later, a helicopter bombed and killed him.

"Pourquoi?" she asked me in French. Why? We talked about how it would have been easier if the man had died before being operated on. He suffered so much more from her help.

A six-year-old tiny, shrunken boy was lying on a table with a white bandage on his stump. Earlier in the day, one of the French doctors had amputated his leg. He had stepped on a shiny, green, plastic bird-like toy, a mine. The Soviets threw thousands of these anti-personnel mines out of their helicopters hoping kids, villagers, or a mujahedeen would pick them up or trip on them and blow up an arm or leg, maiming them for life. The Panjshir people had suffered from war, sieges, starvation. Their eyes showed the deadness, the terror, the exhaustion. Supplies and help were available in this tiny clinic, but it was such little help for the deep wounds they had endured.

* * *

Nearly three weeks had passed since we left Pakistan. In a gathering at a commander's home, as we sat on cushions and drank tea, a young boy ran into the living room and saw John, a foreigner. Something snapped in this boy's mind. He grabbed the Enfield rifle propped against the door and pointed the gun at John's head, ready to shoot him. In an instant, a mujahedeen jumped up and snatched the gun, then shooed the boy out the door.

This boy was one of the runners who brought messages to Massoud. He was an orphan and had seen his parents killed in front of him, during one of the Soviet bombings on his village. The mujahedeen adopted him because he had no family left alive to take care of him. He was a warrior child, sent on dangerous missions moving between enemy lines, bringing chits with coded military messages. Children like him were ideal for this runner job. They were not easy to detect and could run fast from one location to another.

These warrior children, who had been terrorized by what they had seen and been through, would be more open to fundamentalist ideals when they grew up. The Taliban would promise glory for them if they strapped on explosives and died in a suicide bombing. In the 1980s, it was unheard of for an Afghan to be killed in a jihadist suicide. The repercussions of long-term war made the world less safe, rather than safer. After the U.S. invaded Afghanistan on October 7th, 2001, the Afghans came to hate the Americans as they had the Soviets. The fundamentalists now had a new generation of recruits who wanted to attack our soldiers, making terrorism more likely.

* * *

The taxi ride from Teri Mangal to Parachinar then to Peshawar was a blur. We arrived at Green's Hotel in the center of town. Fawad, John, and I checked into two rooms.

Once in my hotel room, I stripped off my filthy clothes. I felt skinnier. My body was twenty pounds lighter. This was a diet I could not recommend to most people: Go to a war zone and survive on whatever you can find. I stepped into the hot shower, layers of dirt washed off. Baba Fawad entered, naked, pressed himself against me, water pounding on our heads. I clung to him. He took me like the first time, my legs wrapped around his waist. He leaned against the shower stall, the water cleansing us, nourishing us, restoring us. I wanted this man in my life. I imagined him walking down the streets of Manhattan, my lover, charming, although out of place, among the skyscrapers. I was not ready to let him go. I loved Baba Fawad, his strength, his confidence, his male foreignness.

"Would you like to live in New York with me?" I asked.

He stared into my eyes, his longing for me felt as intense as mine was for him.

"Yes," he said.

"I will do my best to bring you to New York," I promised.

I wanted to be with him, and I knew he wanted to be with me. It was hard to be rational when in love. All I knew was that I didn't want to lose what I had found.

While John was sleeping, Baba Fawad and I traveled through the markets in Peshawar. As bustling traffic, cars honking, overloaded carts drawn by tired donkeys, and motorized rickshaws whirled through the labyrinth-like streets, Baba Fawad and I walked arm and arm. We passed rose water pudding in large metal bowls cooled on ice and smelled roasted meat kebabs on charcoals. Then, we climbed up the stairs to a second floor restaurant overlooking the third world urban scene below. We ate spicy organ meat stir fry. My stomach, hardened, could digest almost anything now.

After dinner, Baba Fawad took me to a rug shop full of Afghani tribal rugs. In the dark interior, the owner piled one rug on top of the other, showing off their beauty. When the stack was as tall as me, Fawad spoke to the owner in Dari. The owner went into another back room and brought a horse's pack made from an antique Afghani rug. Two large pockets were stitched together with a leather strip in the middle so the bag could slip onto a horse's back.

"It's for you," Baba Fawad told me.

"It is beautiful, a treasure, a memento of our time together," I said.

I never took this present home with me. I told him he could bring it when we met in New York. When I was back in my life in the U.S., I realized my dream of sharing a life with Baba Fawad would not be possible. There were too many obstacles. It was a foolish girl's dream, not to be realized.

* * *

When Fawad and I arrived back at the hotel, satiated, tired, and looking forward to a second shower, the rotund manager spoke to Fawad in Pashtu. Fawad told me he could not stay. The manager told him that mujahedeen were not allowed in the hotel. I was outraged and threatened to call my embassy. This was outright discrimination. We would be leaving, taking our business elsewhere but, first, I wanted to check on John. Fawad waited outside the hotel, while I figured out what to do next.

When I saw John, he was improving from the strain of the climb out of Afghanistan and the symptoms of hepatitis. He thought the British Consulate would have some ideas. I spoke to the Consul, who invited us to stay at his house and sent a car and driver right away to pick us up. Fawad declined the offer and went to stay with his friends in a hostel near the market.

The British colonial splendor at the Consular home was a shocking contrast to some of the dirt floor places where we had stayed in Afghanistan. A Pakistani servant brought a fine china tea set and placed it on an inlayed wood coffee table in front of the Consul, John, and me. Sipping black tea with milk and sugar, while sitting on a silk upholstered couch, John perked up, looking almost like his old self. His yellowed skin began to return to his natural ruddy color.

Joking and displaying his natural wit, John made a good friend of his compatriot. John gave exact reconnaissance, pointed to locations of the government posts, different mujahedeen commanding territories, and abandoned tanks on the detailed topical map provided by the Consul. John was excited when he told the pièce de résistance, the facts about Commander Massoud and the cease-fire in the Panjshir Valley. I listened to the skillful way John gathered, analyzed, and delivered the news. I admired his chutzpah and was grateful that we had made it through thick and thin and arrived at this place of comfort.

The British Consul suggested he would arrange an interview with *The Guardian* newspaper in London. It made me think that I would like a similar interview with *The New York Times* in New York City.

Mostly everything had been forgiven between John and me. Our squabbles were the product of stress, tight nerves, lack of food, and his illness. John planned to stay on a few more days, to recover and enjoy his respite here. I was eager to leave as soon as possible.

The next day, I contacted the American Consulate, expecting similar treatment. On the phone, the American Consul informed me that they had heard of me and that I had overextended my visa. There would be no help from my government. All alone, I took a rickshaw to the American Consulate, a bare, one-room office with a metal desk. I wanted to show the Consul the strategic military locations on the map pinned on the wall. I gave them the names of the commanders who were in charge of the regions. I explained the cease-fire. He seemed uninterested in the information—couldn't care less that I was a freelancer for Dan Rather at CBS. When I told him about Massoud, he didn't know whom I was talking about. I pointed to the Panjshir Valley on the map. He wrote down some notes. I mentioned the Northern Alliance and the Jamiat group. He asked, "Who were they?" I was exasperated with this man.

"You've overextended your one-month visa. This is punishable by a minimum of three months in the local prison." The Consul looked strangely elated at the prospect of me going to a Pakistani jail under his watch.

"Yes, but the British Embassy helps their journalists. So do the French."

"We're not British or French, but American."

Brazen, emboldened, and not about to spend a day in jail, I left the American Consulate and returned to the British Consulate for advice.

"You must get yourself arrested. Then, they will immediately deport you, and you'll be safely back in the U.K. in no time." The British Consul winked at me. No jail time. Perfect. I wasn't planning on coming back to Pakistan anytime in the near future.

After a few phone calls, the British Consul located the Peshawar mayor and gave him a message on my behalf. The mayor was at Green's Hotel for an awards ceremony. I would be returning to the place where Fawad and I had been thrown out.

"Hurry," the Consul told me, "the next flight to London is in four hours. You could still catch it."

Then the English Consulate's driver took me to Green's Hotel. I walked into the lobby with a "nobody-is-going-to-stop-me" attitude. Past the front desk, I handed my bags to the porter, who recognized me. I gave him a sharp look, a wordless "don't-you-dare-get-your-manager" stare. The porter thanked me and took my baggage. In the large interior courtyard, there were lots of well-dressed Pakistani men, some in Western suits and others in traditional pants and tunics, standing around casually. One heavyset man in his fifties in Western dress beckoned me to come over to him.

"You're the American journalist back from the Panjshir Valley," the mayor said.

"Yes."

"Can I have my picture with you?"

"Sure," I replied.

The scene was more like a party than a mission to be deported out of the country. The mayor stood next to me, excited, grinning at the camera. Some other men moved into the picture. The photographer motioned for us to stand closer so as to get everyone in the shot. I told the mayor that my Pakistani visa ran out and I needed to be arrested so I could go home. He smiled, enjoying this saving a damsel in distress moment. His authority unquestioned, he set Pakistani bureaucracy on jet speed and got one of his assistants to take my passport to the nearby office for the deportation stamp. During my fifteen minutes of fame at Green's Hotel, I was officially arrested and made a prisoner of the kind-hearted mayor, who made many special arrangements. He ordered his driver to take me to the Islamabad airport in plenty of time to make my flight to London. No jail time for me.

This lack of care for me by my government proved disheartening. It could have been a fluke, an ill-tempered American Consul, but I was annoyed with the lack of interest, at that time, concerning what was going on inside Afghanistan.

My curiosity about the cease-fire had come full circle. All of my questions were answered. Our story was shot and ready to be edited and broadcast worldwide.

CHAPTER 6
TELLING THE STORY

In late December of 1983, I entered *The New York Times* building, a block north of the Port Authority on 43rd street. Security was lax, and I went straight up to meet Scott Johnson who had asked to interview me about my trip to Afghanistan. His office looked over 8th Avenue, a seedy part of town, where electronics stores advertised going out of business sales as a ploy to sell new cameras. Johnson's door was open, and I walked right into his office. He was dressed in a grey suit and tie, which made him look older than his prep school face. I thought he couldn't have been older than his late twenties.

Scott introduced himself by his first name, adding that he had found me through the AP wire. Then, he eagerly launched into questions about my trip to Afghanistan, taking notes on a steno pad and smiling a lot. He wrote down the facts about Commander Massoud, the Panjshir Valley, the cease fire, Istalif, the bombings, etc. He seemed intrigued by the idea of a woman war journalist, and he wanted to know if I had any photos he could run with the article. I dug into my backpack and took out the clear plastic sheet with slides that John and I had shot. Scott selected the one of me and Fawad on horses leaving the Panjshir Valley.

"When do you think the article will come out?" I asked.

"I'm aiming for as close to the fourth anniversary of the Soviet Invasion as I can get."

"That's good because maybe CBS will change their mind," I said.

Earlier in the day, I had dropped off over four hours of Super 8 footage transferred to Betacam tapes at the reception desk of the CBS producer. His secretary came out to the lobby and told me that the cease-fire story did not conform to what CBS was looking for. I didn't have a chance to meet with the CBS producer to make my case. I hoped that once *The New York Times* article was published, CBS would reconsider its decision.

After the interview, I boarded the train at Penn Station for D.C. I was traveling light. Everything I had was in my backpack. I would be home in time for Christmas.

* * *

When I walked in the door of my mother's townhouse, she was on the phone, checking to see if we needed dinner reservations for an early Christmas celebration. I hugged her awkwardly. She wasn't really a hugger. I would be having two Christmases: one with her and my siblings in D.C., another with my father and his new wife and in-laws in New Jersey. I was already exhausted from all the travel and was not looking forward to shuffling from one place to another, each home feeling less and less like my family home.

The first Christmas dinner, four days before December 25th, was in the oak-paneled Hay Adams Hotel dining room, a block from the White House. My sister, brother, mother, and I were sitting around a table set with silver and crystal glasses for a five-course meal. I was the talker, bragging about my Afghanistan stories.

"There was this one time John used a compass, while we followed Fawad, who was in charge. There was only a small group of us, maybe only four mujahedeen. I couldn't fathom why John thought he could help using his compass. He didn't even have a map. But, anyway, we walked into the center of this village, an open space, surrounded by walled-in compounds. I turned around and there was a Soviet tank parked on a dirt road. You should have seen the surprise on John's face. Whoa! So Fawad quickly turned us around and we retraced our steps right out of town. I don't know what would have happened, if we didn't see that tank before the soldiers came out."

My sister, Elena, looking more somber in her newly dyed black hair, didn't say a word. I was never sure if she was listening to me or her own mind, dreaming of her future life, far away from all of us. We shared a history but had different ways of coping. I often used food to numb myself. She spaced into her own world.

My mother ordered her first martini for the night, extra dry with a pickled onion. She pulled out colorful silk yarn from her leather chestnut brown Coach bag and knitted while having a mumbling conversation with herself. "It's taking too long for the waiter to get my drink. I don't see the Maryland crab cakes on the menu, anymore. Shame, really," she said. "Wolfgang, have you decided what you want for dinner?"

My brother, Wolfgang hid his acned face behind a sci-fi book an inch away from his nose and ignored my mother's questions and my monologue. I couldn't tell if he was truly immune or whether his way of coping was effective. He would bury himself in fantasy books, which kept my mother at a distance and improved his speed reading skills. When the second martini arrived, my brother, still wearing his paperback book in front of his face, sighed and stated, "I'm hungry."

"This is ridiculous, no food yet, and we've been here for half an hour already," my mother said.

The waiter apologized to my mother—some problem with the chef not arriving on time.

"Then bring me a bottle of red wine," my mother said.

The longer we stayed for dinner, the greater the chance of a scene. My mother would pick a fight with me or with the waiter.

Wolfgang and Elena were underage and drank Coke. I drank the red wine in one long gulp. Drinking calmed me, numbed my pain, as it probably did the same for my mother, at first. But where was the line between enjoying drinking and being addicted to drinking? My mother had crossed the line years ago. Nobody in our family but her was known as an alcoholic.

The waiter poured me another glass of wine, avoiding eye contact with my mother. Forty-five minutes later, we still had no real food. Wolfgang inhaled the complementary cornmeal hushpuppies. My mother warned me not to eat the fried hors d'oeuvre. Too many calories. The main chef never showed up.

After many more apologies from the waiter and my third glass of red wine, I stood up and aimed my body in the direction of the bathroom. My first bull's-eye target was to reach the pillars at the dining room entrance without losing my balance. Second, I had to shoot for the chintz floral sofa in the hotel lobby, and third, my final goal was the ladies' room. When I returned from the obstacle course, there was still no entree, and the service was non-existent. The waiter avoided our table; he had run out of excuses.

We left after paying for the drinks and picked up Chinese takeout on the way home. I went to bed early. My mother drank vodka late into the night. No scene happened. We were just a hungry family eating Christmas dinner out of take-out boxes.

* * *

In the morning, I stood at the kitchen counter, eating a toasted English muffin without butter, sipping a cup of extra bitter black coffee without milk, to save on calories. My mother, dressed for work in a wool suit, showed no sign of yesterday's vodka binge. She drank a cup of black coffee.

"Missy, who did you call at Wolfgang's school? Mr. Sullivan left a message that he wanted to speak to me. What are you trying to prove?"

"Mom, please, he's Wolfgang's counselor."

I had contacted the after-school Alateen, an Al-Anon spin-off for teenagers, during the previous summer, the day after I found my mother passed out on the sofa and couldn't get her up. I had called the medics, and, as soon as they arrived, my mother acted as if nothing was the matter. This was crazy-making. So, I enrolled Wolfgang in the after-school counseling program before I left for Afghanistan. With me gone, the counselor was to check up on the situation at home.

My mother didn't care for AA after her detox at the Betty Ford Center. She couldn't believe in the twelve-step program and, not surprisingly, didn't stay sober for long, either. With evangelical zeal, I had staged an intervention, the summer of the yellow couch incident. My mother, sister, and I went to Rancho Mirage for the family program, all paid for by my mother's Federal Government health insurance plan. My sister and I learned about our co-dependency and how we could be manipulated to support my mother's alcohol problem. My mother stopped drinking for a few weeks in her locked ward. When she returned home, she started up again, with the same intensity. I wanted Wolfgang to learn how he could cope better living with our alcoholic mother.

My mother's demons were medicated and suppressed by alcohol, which kept them at bay internally, but alcoholism is a selfish disease. My mother's desire for alcohol meant she couldn't really attend to the job of motherhood. Home didn't feel safe. At any moment, her rage could gush out. When I was around, her drunken self would charge at me, screaming about things I had done to her. When I was away in London at film school, her temper was more focused on my father, but my brother was now taking the brunt of it. My sister had learned to just not be around. I feared that my brother's tactic of reading paperback sci-fi fiction non-stop in front of my mother would not save him from damage. He was fifteen and vulnerable. My father's new marriage had taken his attention, and there was little help from him for Elena and Wolfgang.

"Mom, this is for Wolfgang to get support around your drinking problem," I said. Denial was not an option. My mother's alcoholism was no longer the elephant in the room. I believed that everything needed to be out in the open, a tenet I held onto in all future intimate relationships. Telling the truth to myself, taking the risk, and saying what I was feeling to the people closest to me was the first step to recovery.

"You're so lazy and take advantage of me all the time. Why are you here? I thought you were leaving for New Jersey to be with your father and that bitch," my mother said. "And what about my American Express card? It's for emergencies only. You used it again!"

My father was picking me up in two days on Christmas Eve. I could have told her this calmly, but my anger was aroused.

"I don't want to talk about this. I have to go," I shouted and left the kitchen.

My body was shaking from fury.

My mother followed me, "I want to have this conversation with you, young lady. You refused to talk to me last night after dinner."

When my mother was drunk, her fallback conversation was a philosophical speech on inductive and deductive logic, which I had heard a hundred times before. "Deductive reasoning arrives at a specific conclusion based on generalizations. Inductive reasoning takes events and makes generalizations," straight from the dictionary and branded in my brain forever.

Her obsession with these ideas, if I could stand the repetition, would eventually lead to whether God existed. She was an atheist who had me and my siblings baptized in the Episcopal Church after my father nearly died in the fire—just in case God did exist. This philosophical question, repeated over and over, infiltrated my cellular being.

There was a choice to look at the world from an inductive or deductive point of view and that choice influenced my work, life, and beliefs. I chose inductive reasoning, believing in my personal experiences more than handed-down dogmas. I felt the power of Source/God/Love/Creator directly from a young age and never doubted its existence. I pursued opportunities to see for myself what was going on and what was true.

However, no deductive or inductive logic, no grace, and no intention came to resolve our conflict. Her quandary about God's existence was an underground current that was contrary to Alcoholics Anonymous' step two of its twelve-step program, "recognizing a higher power that can give strength." She had never told me about a direct experience of God, which I had felt as a little girl. As a little girl, my mother thought God had punished her by killing her father, a wound that festered deep in the unconscious. Now, as an adult she could not believe in God, but wasn't entirely sure, either.

Outside the kitchen, I sneered at my mother and at the thought of having to listen to her definition one more time. She snapped and raised her arm to hit me—our argument was no longer verbal, it was getting physical. I was so mad, I was willing to fight back. I was too young and immature to step back and see a bigger picture. I ran to the bathroom and locked the door, bawling and sobbing.

"You're visiting that woman's parents," shouted my mother, referring to Katherine, my father's new wife.

Sitting on the toilet seat, crying, I plugged my ears with my fingers, while my mother shouted through the locked door. Our relationship was on the verge of ending, just like her own relationship with her mother. They had not spoken for a decade. I took deep breaths, calmed down. My hot throat relaxed and stopped quivering. I didn't want this kind of relationship. I wanted to bridge this gap and not leave this scene hating my mother. Could this be the shift? I was forming a new intention. I was finding a new strength to be calm in the face of my mother's demands.

The intensity of this fight with my mother served to open a door that I hadn't seen before. I no longer wanted the adrenaline of fighting. In Afghanistan, I looked for the story of peace and used my strength to find those scenes and film them. I no longer had to react all the time. My habitual battle mode quieted, and something new suddenly seemed possible. My mother must have felt the calmness that had replaced my anger and anxiety, and this new feeling changed her, too.

"That hurt when you said you plugged your ears," my mother's tone also shifted, becoming more soft and vulnerable.

"I love you. I get that you have all this stuff you have to tell me, but I don't want these conversations to turn negative and against me. I don't want to feel I'm being punished every time we talk. I realize it doesn't work to not have the conversation; It just adds up and adds up until you have to let it out," I said.

I drove my mother to work. We avoided a physical confrontation, reconciled at a new level of understanding. Our connection as mother and daughter was intact.

"Melissa," she said, "I don't want to lose you. We have our problems, and that is OK. I love you. I believe in you, and I'm excited for your new life in New York."

Finally, a breakthrough. My mother stopped accusing me and started supporting me. She even gave me good wishes. I didn't eat much all day and got tons of work done—made phone calls and dropped off a copy of the Afghanistan footage to the United States Information Agency, who bought the film for their archives. I packed for my life in New York City.

The next morning, my mother didn't get up for work and stayed home. I was not sure how she kept her high-powered job at the Federal Reserve Board, writing major government reports on auto sales forecasts, while drinking the way she did. My mother's fifth of vodka was half empty in the freezer, empty glass bottles were in the trash. I was eating again, Pepperidge Farm mint Milanos, Pepperidge Farm 3-Layer frozen German chocolate cake, Häagen-Dazs coffee ice cream: a real binge. I made myself sick, but I was OK. I would try to get back on a diet, even though it was the holidays.

Food was a source of pleasure and pain. I could feel secure, sitting on the couch, eating ice cream, and watching TV. Then came the guilt, self-hatred, and feelings of lack of beauty, lack of love, lack of friends. In Afghanistan, survival was so basic that my food issues were non-existent, but back in D.C., those issues resurfaced. The flow I experienced in Afghanistan stopped, and now I was turned against myself, generating negative momentum.

The up and down reactions to life were more polarized when serious addictions were involved. Self-nurturing methods veered toward the harmful: alcohol for my mother, and food for me. I sensed we both felt shame when pushed to use our drug of choice, and we blamed life's dramas to justify their use.

* * *

I called George in Greece. Through the crackly long distance phone lines, super conscious of the cost per minute of the call, I confessed: "I had a really big fight with Mom. It's OK, we worked it out in the end." My voice echoing, as I spoke to George.

"Sweetie, your mother loves you. She wants the best for you," he said. "When are you coming?"

"I want to be with you, hold you, make love to you," I said.

"So come."

"I can't. I'm going to stay with Sarah in New York and work on *Big Red*. Remember the puppet film about the Soviet Union?"

"I'll wait for you," he said. "I love you absolutely."

It was the first time he said "absolutely." I was stunned by this word. I cried. What did it mean to be loved absolutely? I didn't love myself absolutely. I force-fed myself to go numb, like my mother with her alcohol. That was not love.

George's love soothed me, gave me a layer of self-esteem, and diffused my crazy, destructive self.

George was an anchor in my life. His attentiveness and joy were my support. I looked forward to our life together when he finished his military service and moved to the States to be with me.

* * *

On Christmas Eve morning, my father was waiting to pick me up outside my mother's house in a blue Chrysler K car. He usually drove a more luxurious car, a Porsche, a Cadillac, even a Maserati at one point. He was building up his life, after what I called a "vow of poverty," when my mother left him penniless. He had Clark Kent blue eyes and wore a leather flight jacket and baggy pants. His wife was already in New Jersey with her family. It was unusually warm for late December. The sun was shining for our father-daughter drive north.

I inserted the seat belt clasp around my waist. The law didn't require wearing seat belts, but my mother always insisted. My father didn't wear his.

"Did you see the two Buddhas of Bamiyan when you were in Afghanistan this time? They were carved in the side of a cliff over 1,400 years ago, and they're more than 170 feet tall. There is Vairocana, the Buddha that is the embodiment of Emptiness. And Shakyamuni is the Buddha we know, the enlightened one," my father said.

"No, I must have been close to them, but didn't have the chance," I told my father. Years later, in 2001, the Taliban dynamited and destroyed both Buddhas, claiming they were idols and evil.

I changed the subject, "I don't think CBS is going to broadcast my footage. I'm really upset." I explained the circumstances and what I went through to get the story. My father stared ahead, as he navigated out of D.C., shifting gears frequently until he reached 80 mph on Interstate 95 to New Jersey. I talked for a long time, while he listened. I told the G-rated version of my adventure in the northern part of Afghanistan.

"Suffering comes from attachments," he said. "Everything is impermanence. Nothing matters when you understand how the universe works."

I understood what my father meant. There must be a place beyond attachments and desire: an acceptance of impermanence. This was the core experience of Buddha's enlightenment. CBS didn't matter in my father's cosmos.

"When I left Afghanistan the first time," I said. "I tasted an intense, euphoric, otherworldly experience. I became a particle of everything around me. I exploded into the mountains, the car, the road, the sky, the sun. It was like I was a part of It, maybe God. For sure Source."

My father nodded. He pointed to the passing trees outside the window and didn't say a word. We'd had these moments in the past, and I knew what he meant by this simple gesture. We were this and this and this … Nothing more.

My father met his Zen teacher when I left for London to go to film school. For years, he immersed himself in the Buddhist teachings and intense meditation, attending the seven-day sesshins every two months at Dai Bosatsu Zendo in New York's Catskills. I knew these teachings encouraged detachment, self-realization, and going beyond the ego, but I was struggling with daily life.

"And Mom is much worse. Her drinking is constant. I'm worried about Elena and Wolfgang."

"Remember, life is an illusion, Missy. Nothing is real. Once you can go beyond dualistic notions, you can see that there is no pain or evil," he said.

"But they didn't ask for these troubles."

"Who is it that did not ask to be born before our father and mother conceived us? This self is an idea and can be disastrous if identified with your real nature. There is only the totality of what is," my father said. Relief would not come from action, he implied. My father's hands-off Zen approach was hard to comprehend.

My direct experience of an ecstatic state, an alternate reality, pointed to an existence that was not about succeeding on earthly terms. It was more about connecting beyond time and space, going beyond. My father's early morning chant: "Gate, Gate, Paragate, Parasamgate, Bodhi, Svaha," the Heart Sutra—Gone, Gone, Gone beyond, Gone beyond, Awakening, So be it—touched something deep in my soul. I trusted the Zen precepts, the dharma, and what I could learn as the daughter of a Zen master, I just didn't know how to apply these teachings in real life.

* * *

After Christmas, my father drove me to New York to live with my friend, Sarah, at her loft in Soho.

"Dad, wait till you see how arty Sarah's loft is. There's no buzzer or intercom, only a broken doorbell hanging from a wire. I'll have to call her from the payphone so she knows it's us. Then she'll drop the front door key in a sock," I told him, as we exited the Holland Tunnel and drove down West Broadway to Broome Street.

The previous spring, after visiting George in Greece and several months before leaving with John for Afghanistan, I met Sarah Peterson for the first time. That day, the sun shone on puddles formed after a quick shower on the wide avenue in Soho. I walked down Broadway, past an office supply store with dusty old typewriters on display, past a fabric store with bolts of upholstery leaning against the entrance, to the corner of Broome Street. I turned right at the Puerto Rican fast food joint that smelled of fried churros. The once elegant iron buildings were covered in grey soot. The streets were empty. I was elated to discover a new neighborhood in Manhattan that I hadn't seen before.

Sarah was a filmmaker working on a puppet animation film about her journey on the Trans-Siberian railroad across the U.S.S.R. She had placed a tiny ad in *The Independent*, a film magazine for independent filmmakers, looking for a producer for her film, and I was applying for the position.

I rang the then-working doorbell that hung from a dangling wire out of the sixth floor window in what had once been an old shoe factory. Sarah was expecting me. She shouted, "Watch out," as she threw down a sock with the front door key in it. This was Soho pre-galleries, pre-designer stores, and pre-chic restaurants. Sarah was one of the early artists to rent a loft with roommates, a Soho pioneer.

The red wool sock bounced like a tennis ball on the sidewalk and rolled under a parked car. I retrieved the key, opened the heavy metal door, and climbed an endless number of dirty stairs. Panting, I arrived at another large metal door, spray painted electric blue with a hippie-style number 6 in day glow orange.

Sarah turned the knob on the crossbar police lock and pushed the squeaky door open. Her smile revealed her perfect, shiny white teeth. She wore a soft, red cotton blouse, exposing a little cleavage, tucked into military green khaki pants. Sarah commanded attention softly but energetically, talking non-stop and not finishing her sentences. She had the air of a revolutionary about her. She wore a black beret that reminded me of Che Guevara.

Sarah's studio was in the front of the loft—800 square feet of open space with two large windows covered in plastic for the winter, both facing the World Trade Center, and one smaller window, uncovered, facing West toward the Holland Tunnel. I had entered into an atelier of another century when there were minstrel puppet shows. Sarah asked me if I wanted a cup of coffee. She had made a fresh pot. "Milk, no sugar," I told her.

I looked at the Big Red train displayed in the open space against a brick wall, while Sarah brought a cup of creamy coffee. She had recreated the Trans-Siberian train car she traveled in during the 1980 summer boycott of the Moscow Olympics. Sarah took the puppet of herself off its perch on the train roof. The oil-painted, sculpted face stared back at me with the same mouth, the big beautiful teeth, and wearing clothes identical to her creator's. The Sarah puppet even wore a black beret and, casually tucked under the hat, was a lock of Sarah's real, ash-brown hair.

"I was the only American on the train. These people treated me like a friend; we liked each other. We were not that different after all. So, when I came home, I locked myself in the loft for eight days, ate the same food as what I ate on the train—lots of borscht and drank strong black tea. I made the train and the puppets, all recreations of the people I met. I even shot the film just to show that they're like us," she told me.

"This is a radical idea," I said. "President Reagan gives so many speeches about how the Soviets are the evil of the modern world. There is so much Cold War rhetoric and anti-communist propaganda: The Soviets are the Evil Empire because of the nuclear build-up. What kind of difference do you think your film will make? There is so little sympathy for them." I didn't share her sentiments that the Soviets could be our friends. This meeting with Sarah took place months before I met Massoud and heard of his desire for peace with the Soviet Union.

Sarah removed the roof of the four-foot-tall papier-mâché train. We peered down at the Tea Lady carrying a tray of Russian tea glasses in silver filigree tea glass holders. She was twice the size of the Sarah puppet, and her breasts were bursting out of her muddy green uniform. She stood next to a samovar replica that Sarah had built inside her train.

Sarah removed the Tea Lady and cradled her on her lap, like a ventriloquist with her dummy. The puppet took on its own individual personality.

"The Tea Lady serves tea to the passengers on the Trans-Siberian. She suffered so much during the Leningrad siege in WWII. There was no food. The Nazis were blocking any supplies from entering the city."

"Really? How awful. How long did the blockade last?"

"900 days."

My reaction to this Communist, ogre-like face softened after I learned of her plight. The Tea Lady puppet had anthropomorphized through Sarah's stories.

"The Tea Lady's main job on the train was to keep the seven-day, 6,152-mile train ride from Vladivostok to Moscow on schedule. She would wag her finger at me, if I didn't get back on the train quick enough at the stations. But there were delays, anyway. My trip ended up being eight-days, after all," Sarah said.

"You're really fond of this Tea Lady. Do you think this puppet can change the mind of Americans? She's a communist worker. Can you make her seem more human to us? Make us understand her better?"

Sarah nodded then went back to the kitchen to get us both another cup of hot coffee. I stood by myself next to the *Big Red* train and reached over to pick up Alexi, a handsome Soviet naval officer. I felt like the puppet morphed into a miniature sailor who flirted with me. Sarah returned with the coffee and told me that he came from a village near Novosibirsk. Then, there was Natasha, the young gymnast, who asked lots of questions in broken English about life in the United States.

"She was my favorite," Sarah said. "Strong but sweet, too. And the Americans love the gymnasts. She'll be a star in my film."

Sarah was clearly breaking with her contemporaries, who were part of the minimalist and postmodern movements, where everything was a derivative of something else. She had transitioned into more personal work. For one of her series, she made large charcoal drawings of dental plates of her teeth; dentists purchased them for their offices. But this puppet thing was a big leap in the artistic community.

In the film she showed me, on a borrowed 16mm viewer, hand-cranked, no sound, her puppets broke into spontaneous dancing in the train aisle. I had to imagine the Soviet disco in the background. The string puppets bumped into each other, chest to chest, and toasted their everlasting friendships. The film was comical and enchanting. Sarah played Tchaikovsky's "Dance of the Sugar Plum Fairy" on her Walkman, the music tinny through the small speaker. I watched as the *Big Red* train flew off its rails through the painted midnight Siberian sky.

This film, the puppets, the train were original, birthed from an artist's imagination. I was mesmerized by the film's power to seduce me with its images, colors, and delight. The message, combined with the form, was unique and conveyed the humanity of the Soviet people. I was emotionally hooked into these characters and Sarah's dream of making a feature film. We could not risk a war with these people. I saw what I could not see in Afghanistan on my first trip: The Soviets were not very different from us.

Sarah made a third pot of fresh coffee and asked about me. I told her about filming in Afghanistan with the mujahedeen, about film school in London, and how my fiancé George was stuck in the Greek Navy.

It was getting dark out, hours had passed, and the loft was cold. The March winds blew outside the brick walls of the 3,000-square-foot loft space. I noticed that there were four bedrooms next to Sarah's large studio. We drank cup after cup of hot coffee, which kept our hands warm.

"Do you think you could be president of the United States?" Sarah asked me, as I was preparing to leave. Apparently, she asked this of all the candidates she interviewed to be her producer.

"Yes," I didn't hesitate, even though I was surprised by the question. Later, Sarah would tell me that I'd been the only interviewee who gave an affirmative answer. It wasn't that I wanted to be president, but the idea of being a powerful woman who could lead people felt possible.

Despite my agony about my weight, I knew I had enough inner confidence to inspire others and wanted to make a difference in the world. I would step forward, seeking a way to lead, while my inner critic ranted: "You are not good enough." This repeated thought of not being good enough surfaced whenever I was ready to leap into the new, the unknown, and the next. I eventually learned to ignore the thought, but in my twenties, the curse still had a hold on me.

Sarah offered me the no-pay, raise-your-own-funds producer position for Big Red Productions. I was honored to have this job and a new purpose in my life, a bigger vision to focus on.

Outside Sarah's loft window, the sun was setting over the Holland Tunnel, and a giant billboard advertising Calvin Klein men's underwear lit up. Male genitals, hidden behind cloth, dominated the Soho block, while two women in a loft made plans to change the world.

I didn't leave after I accepted the new job. Instead, we snacked on cheese and crackers and continued to talk late into the evening about war, peace, feminism, and how artists had a responsibility to make their audiences pay attention, to wake them up. Women had the answer because they knew how much people suffered in life, especially in wars. Our voices needed to be heard.

Late, well past 11 p.m. and hurrying to catch the last bus to New Jersey, where I was staying, I staggered down the six flights onto the empty, artificially lit streets of Soho. I turned around and faced the opposite direction from where I needed to go. I walked past the traffic triangle across from Broome Street smack into the entrance of the Holland Tunnel, a tight place, where an inclined road dove into the tunnel, tumbling into an Alice in Wonderland-type rabbit hole.

Like Alice, I felt a new adventure was beginning. Sarah's mystery made me wonder, "Who was this powerful woman?" I had been enticed by the magical spell of Sarah's life. We had set a date to meet again in a few days.

"Watch out!" I heard Sarah shout as the key wrapped in a sock bounced in front of my father and me, a few days before the 1984 New Year and nine months after I first met her and took the producer job. My father gave me a quick hug then raced uptown to his business meeting in mid-town, leaving me and my bags on the street.

After I came back from my second trip to Afghanistan, Sarah had invited me to move in and sleep in her bedroom—on the white rattan bed, below her loft bed. Being roommates cemented our partnership. Sarah and I shared ideals, methods, and courage. A new course of events would follow, and it all felt right. In Afghanistan, I had been propelled by a sense of danger and adventure; now, I shared a mission and a goal to produce *Big Red*. The film would inspire viewers to see the Soviet Union in a different light, a friendly gesture towards peace.

* * *

A cold draft blew through the brick walls of Sarah's sixth floor loft. The kitchen was the warmest room. Mice scurried across the kitchen counters, ducked into the stove's burners, and left black pellets on the shelves. The sun streamed through the plastic-covered windows that faced the World Trade Towers in the distance. It was Tuesday morning, December 27th, 1983, the day after *The New York Times* printed the article about my trip to the Panjshir Valley. The indestructible rotary dial phone rang in the hallway. Sarah answered it.

"It's for you," Sarah said, half awake.

The base of the black phone fell on the floor, when she handed me the receiver. I dragged the phone on the floor by its curled wire so it could reach me at the kitchen table. The voice on the other end was professional and straight to the point. He was a producer at CNN and wanted an interview about the war in Afghanistan. How soon could I meet him? Did I have any footage they could broadcast?

In *The New York Times'* black and white photo, Fawad and I were riding horses. I was wearing the sheepskin vest Fawad gave me. The article was published in the Metro section. But this was international news! Clearly, the reporter had not understood the point I was trying to make or was dissing me, either because I was a woman journalist or the paper wanted to bury the cease-fire story far from the front page as a human interest piece. I was also peeved that the newspaper insisted on calling me "Miss Burch," announcing my marital status when they quoted me. I had argued with Scott, the staff writer, that he could use "Ms. Burch," instead. He said it was against company policy.

"Wow," Sarah said, when I hung up. "They want you on cable."

I was more nonchalant after my experience with CBS. Dan Rather was no longer interested in the cease-fire story. The CBS producers thought the news story was too complicated. They wanted a simple David and Goliath war story. The Afghans were the underdog fighting a Super Power. The idea of diplomacy or any kind of negotiations to resolve conflict between the Soviet Union and Afghanistan was not compatible with CBS's agenda at that time. So they passed on my footage.

However, the BBC had been thrilled with our work. They dedicated ten minutes on BBC Newsnight to in-depth coverage of Commander Massoud and the Panjshir Valley cease-fire for British audiences. American TV audiences would be kept in the dark.

The phone rang again. Sarah answered it and handed me the phone base and receiver together. It was the same producer as before. He sounded less formal and more edgy.

"What will you talk about?" he asked.

"Commander Massoud. He negotiated a cease-fire in the Panjshir Valley with the Soviet army. It's a first. Both sides walk freely, out in the open. Massoud trains his mujahedeen right under the noses of the Afghan government post."

"I see," he answered and sounded deflated. "Anything else?"

"Yes, in Istalif, a beautiful village totally untouched by war until my partner and I got there, fourteen people were killed. Their houses were bombed because the Soviets found out they were hiding journalists. I found out about all the deaths after I left Istalif."

"OK," was his simple non-committal reply. I had heard the same tone from the secretary of the producer at CBS. It would be a no-go. They wanted this war to look like the Soviets' Vietnam. They didn't want to know that villages were bombed because of journalists visiting. The peace story involved too much explaining. Who was Commander Massoud? Where was the Panjshir Valley? Why was this cease-fire important? My plan to affect global policy by broadcasting a news story about peace had been naïve.

"Same old, same old. I've had it with network news. It's not possible to get the truth out. Too much censorship from the top," I said to Sarah, who was sitting at the kitchen table drinking coffee. There was the difficulty of finding the story and filming it but, without distribution, it was like the Zen koan, "Did the tree fall in the forest if nobody heard it?"

"What are you going to do?" Sarah asked, while she got up and poured herself another cup of coffee.

"It's over. News is too controlled. It's impossible to get the truth out here about this war," I said.

Anne, one of Sarah's five roommates, walked into the kitchen and poured herself a cup of black coffee. Tall and thin, she sat down on the stool next to me. Her long scarves trailed on the dirty wooden floor. Black eyeliner completely encircled her eyes—protection from demons, she claimed.

"Art is where you can tell the truth. It's where the eyewitness can deliver what matters. It is the power of your voice, your journey, your adventure, your convictions that must get out," said Anne. She was an artist and philosopher. She loved to give sermons, political speeches as the MC at the East Village Pyramid Club, which she co-founded for gay men as a place where they could celebrate life and differences.

Then we sat in silence.

I had believed journalism was about the truth of the story, could inspire people to change, to make a difference. Now, I understood that the gatekeepers in news-making controlled the message so that it was nearly impossible for news to be a catalyst. Art was where I would have more freedom and could tell the story. My limitation would be finding the money I needed.

Sarah, Anne, and I sat around the kitchen table, the scarred wooden table full of black rings from sweating glasses and hot pans, the epicenter of our sixth floor loft and female-driven artist community.

"Yes, that is what we need to do. Make a place where your story can be told, where nobody can stop you. Women artists must have a place they can call their own, like Virginia Woolf's room of one's own. You have to tell about what is really going on in Afghanistan, what nobody sees on the news," said Sarah.

Anne leaned forward balancing her waif-like frame on the metal stool.

Sarah started to plan a place for women artists to tell the truth and share their work in a public place.

"When Sally wakes up, we can ask her about a gallery space in the East Village where they are looking for alternative events. I think it's called the Limbo Lounge. The owner is a friend of hers. Maybe we could use that space," Anne was referring to another roommate, Sally, a Vidal Sassoon hair colorist, who had been out late partying the night before.

"Perfect," Sarah said. "I'll ask her as soon as she wakes up."

The synergy of the women at the loft made it seem like we had solutions for everything. We were more than the sum of the parts. Working together, inspired by each other, we created new possibilities.

* * *

Near Tompkins Square Park in Manhattan's Alphabet City, where heroin addicts, drunks, and homeless people camped out, there was a new group of women artists who gathered on Sunday afternoons at the Limbo Lounge storefront art gallery and club. "Art galleries are multiplying like white rats," said one art critic about what was happening in the East Village in 1984. WOW Cafe Theater, a lesbian performance art group, opened next door to the Limbo Lounge.

Sarah, her loft roommates, women artist friends, and I organized talks, performances, and art shows at the Limbo Lounge. One artist created a poster with women in halos dancing the limbo. The name stuck, Women in Limbo. We, the women artists, felt like we were in limbo, not mainstream, too serious for the East Village fun art, not serious enough for the members of the feminist art academics, not postmodernists but more expressionistic, autobiographical, political, and globally conscious. We were multi-media artists, combining forms, using film, sculpture, painting, and performance, when art critics frowned on this practice. We were not all lesbians, we did not identify ourselves based on our sexuality, but we were not afraid to call ourselves feminists.

In February of 1984, Sarah projected her ten-minute 16mm puppet animation film, Journey on the Trans-Siberian Express, on the Limbo Lounge gallery wall.

We had a space of our own.

* * *

On a cold April day, Sarah and I walked from the loft to First Avenue, then over to Eleventh Street. It was a couple of miles. We walked everywhere to save money. We collected all the coins we had to pay for lunch. We bought chicken wings for less than a dollar or two. We were on a tight budget, making the money from the international sales of my Afghanistan footage last as long as possible.

In the white gallery room at the Limbo Lounge, I set up the TV and VCR and showed the BBC documentary about the Panjshir Valley. The 20-minute video had never been shown in the States before, but it had been broadcast in many countries besides the

United Kingdom, including Germany and Japan. The images flashed on the big screen: the buzkashi game, horses charging each other, Commander Massoud signing chits on the hood of his Russian car. The English narrator explained how the ceasefire had brought peace to the region.

"Massoud has a vision of a united, independent country. He believes in equality for men and women, religious tolerance and democracy," my voice rose, breathless. "He's also a Sufi Master." I spoke in front of twenty or more women about Massoud and my experiences in Afghanistan. The irony was that a CBS broadcast could reach millions but, here, I felt listened to, understood, and accepted. The screening was genuine, important, and beneficial. I made a difference here at the Limbo Lounge. I could be a role model for other women to follow their passions and take risks, even if there would be no guarantees of success.

"My story began when I first went to Afghanistan at 21 years old. I didn't know anything about the history or politics of this country. I did what I thought I should do, shoot battle footage for a major network. It was well-received and fit the agenda of the times. It was a simple story, a small band of guerrilla soldiers fighting the big bad Soviets."

I continued, "Afghanistan is a country that will not surrender. They are like us women artists. We cannot be co-opted, we cannot be deceived, we must work to tell the truth and show what is really going on."

I had found my voice. I told the women how I felt guilty about the deaths that were caused by my being there.

"On my second trip, I was much more experienced. I had a mission to show the possibilities and potential for peace and introduce the commander that could make a difference. CBS and CNN would not show the story about Commander Massoud and the Panjshir Valley. *The New York Times* put the article in the Metro section. News organizations are owned by big corporations with ties to the government. They want to show the Afghans nipping at the Soviets' heels, a Soviet version of the Vietnam propaganda story," I told the women.

"People think the news is unbiased, only facts, and that it keeps you informed about what is going on. Think again. You get only what they, the establishment, want you to know, to keep you in the rat race, distracted and confused by who got whom pregnant in celebrity circles, so that you won't question or protest the wars or escalating nuclear weapons against the Soviet Union, despite whatever treaties exist."

I had found a platform. Maybe it was just a drop in the ocean, but the ripple effects could be like the butterfly wing that could affect the weather thousands of miles away. I was shifting consciousness bit by bit.

"We must work together. We must make art and independent films where we have freedom of expression. No one can take our creativity away from us. We need your feminist perspective, not another Hollywood bimbo representing us or a soap detergent ad that proclaims the virtues of women washing clothes. We have to be smart, use our deep understanding, self-expression, and courage to show what is true for you and for me."

In front of this small audience, I became a leader. I could inspire and chart a course. Sarah recognized this aspect in me when we first met. Here I was, passionate about a cause and willing to stand up and encourage others to join.

Sarah stood up after me and spoke about the Cold War propaganda, "Do we know the truth about the Soviet Union? Who are the Soviet people? We're told they are monsters because they are communists. I had to hide under a desk in my Milwaukee grade school, in case of a Soviet nuclear bomb attack. My desk could not protect me. This is nonsense."

Many of the women at the Limbo Lounge remembered the Cuban Missile Crisis and how close we came to nuclear war.

"We must understand who they are, the Soviets, the people. They have hopes and dreams like us. We cannot believe what our government wants us to believe. We must see for ourselves," said Sarah.

I believed in the *Big Red* message. We would show the human side of the Soviets, to avoid nuclear war. I believed this in my heart. Sarah envisioned using puppets, a simple story, a journey to meet real people, captured on film. When you had a relationship with someone, it would be harder to see them as the enemy. It would be harder to kill them. This wisdom would be shared through the power of art.

In this small group of feminist artists, the energy was palpable, akin to dandelion seeds blowing on fertile ground. The women came up afterwards to thank us for the presentations. And they wanted to be sure that Women in Limbo would keep meeting. We would find a way to support women artists to have a voice, to share their personal experiences, to make a difference in the world. Feminists had declared that the personal was political. This must be true in art, as well as in our lives. *Big Red* was the way Sarah and I would achieve this change, but we wanted all women artists to act boldly, take their work seriously, use their voices, and send their message out into the public.

The energetic impulse to connect to a vision was like oxygen. I had to live this principle, even when it became difficult, even when I would have to suffer through failures to find a way to create change. I saw that an artist could operate without restraints and on her own terms. I yearned to go forward to produce original work that could shift society, evolve old ways, and create new solutions.

The author – Kandahar, Afghanistan, 1982

The author with mujahedeen in Afghanistan

Afghani women in Afghanistan

Commander Shah Massoud in Panjshir Valley

The author's mother

George, the author's husband

The author's father

THIRD PART

PURPOSEFUL AND REFINED ACTION

"Behind all her cruel sporting with human fate, there lies something like a hidden purpose."

~ C.G. Jung

CHAPTER 7

LOVE TRIANGLE

"What is that smell?" Sarah asked, "Is there a dead mouse in the room?"

We started to remove suitcases and bags of clothes from under the loft bed in Sarah's bedroom.

"It's coming from over here," I said.

I opened a ripped garbage bag and the skunked smell seeped out. It was the sheepskin vest from Fawad.

"Do you think the smell will go away if I dry clean it?" I asked.

"You can try," Sarah said.

I had been in New York for several months, and I couldn't imagine my Afghan warrior adapting to life in the big city. The Afghans in New York drove taxis, which didn't seem like the life for Fawad. Afghanistan seemed like a distant world—rugged, earthy, sensual—compared to life in New York, which was fast-paced, heady.

Fawad had made me feel safe. George nurtured me. However, I seemed to be looking for something else—a creative partnership between equals, no more bullshit role playing or projecting my needs onto my significant other. I knew the trappings of emulating or rejecting my parents' values. My parents had stretched gender roles but ultimately failed.

Lately, I had been spending most of my time with Sarah. We lived together, worked together, and went everywhere together, to movies, museums, gallery openings, plays. Little by little, we were becoming inseparable. We talked for hours, late into the night, about women, their roles, our mothers, our sisters, Sylvia Plath, Virginia Woolf, Louise Bourgeois, and Anaïs Nin.

Sarah had a good relationship with her mother, who was an art teacher and encouraged her to be an artist in New York City. I had forged my identity and passions in opposition to my mother, who wanted me to go to an Ivy League college. Smith was her first choice, her alma mater. But I rejected higher education as a path, when I saw how it had not served my mother or her friend and roommate, Sylvia Plath, in finding joy and harmony in their lives. Yet, we were more alike than not—independent, ambitious, courageous, and both wounded in childhood.

Sarah wanted me to reconcile with my mother, and to let her more into my life. She nudged me to call her.

"Mom, I want you to meet Sarah, my girlfriend I told you about. How about us coming to visit you in D.C. real soon?"

The following weekend, Sarah and I carried our duffel bags down the six flights of stairs, walked to the E train on Spring Street, and took the subway to Penn Station. Meandering through the tunnels in the bowels of Manhattan, we waited in line to purchase the round-trip tickets to Washington—charging them on my mother's American Express card. She was now financing more and more of our personal living expenses and the *Big Red* pre-production costs.

I hoped my mother wouldn't erupt about the money, a sore topic for both of us, or talk about her hatred of my father or complain about some minor infraction I had committed. It could be really uncomfortable, if she started on a tirade. My mother could be so unpredictable.

Sarah and I took the escalator down to the platform and boarded the Amtrak train. The train wheels rolled over the tracks, rocking Sarah and me back and forth, as we pulled out of New York City. The late April sun was setting. Horizontal magenta, deep purple, and orange bands crossed the sky. We were set in motion.

I also wanted Sarah to see the mother I idealized. In college, in the 50s, she was one of the first women to be awarded a Marshall Scholarship to Somerville College at Oxford University, which Margaret Thatcher also attended. My mother was a feminist who had gone before us to pave the way, to make it easier for my generation to succeed in the patriarchal world.

I also knew there was a part of me that wanted my mother's attention when I was with her. She was intrigued with my life as an independent filmmaker. She was proud of my trips to Afghanistan and the work I did. And my mother was concerned that it would be difficult to make a living, since I was having trouble making ends meet.

There was a lot of uncertainty, but I felt everything would work out. Sarah and I were surfing a huge wave. The wave of external circumstances existed outside of us, but I knew how to stay balanced on the surfboard: Keep my eyes focused on the horizon, on the goals, and take the necessary steps, no matter what. All this outer directed energy turned into power and into an exhilarating experience. Creativity was the fabric of our beings and experiences.

On the train, I told Sarah about a dream I had the night before. I was on a train like the one we were on. We were on separate trains going to the ocean. I was worried that I wouldn't find her. When we arrived on different trains, standing on different platforms, I saw her enter a small glassed-in station. The two trains we had disembarked from were coupled. We boarded together the joined train and sat across from each other in the dining car. The train left the station and rolled on the surface of the foamy ocean. Sarah and I drank Bud beers out of the can and ate salty peanuts, while the train sped across the vast water.

As our own train sped south towards D.C., I felt a tingling deep inside me. Sarah and I leaned into each other. A juicy impulse rose up, a natural, yet totally forbidden feeling. The interior of the train was covered in shadow. An occasional flashing light pierced the darkness.

Two passengers boarded the train and sat in the bolted chairs in front of us. They tilted their seats back into our cocoon space. I was overcome with desire. Sarah and my lips touched tentatively, my nipples hardened. I was hungry for more. We touched the softest parts of our bodies, cheeks, breasts, thighs. I slipped my hand down her pants. A stickiness between her legs. A gasp. A moan. We were intoxicated from the rocking, the caresses, the cosmic pulse. Exuberance and passion were shooting through every cell of my body.

My mother had moved out of the townhouse in Dupont Circle, her previous residence and the setting for many dramatic moments in our lives, including the yellow couch-washing incident. She had moved back to The Ontario into Apartment 107, the one-bedroom apartment that was saved because my grandmother had bought it in cash for my mother. Apartment 105, next door to 107, partially lost to the kitchen fire, was later fully lost to foreclosure by my father, at a time when banks did not give mortgages to women.

We took a taxi to my mother's place, driving through Rock Creek Park with the windows rolled down. We were intoxicated by the smells of damp leaves and the fresh spring air. We crossed the Duke Ellington Bridge, also known as Suicide Bridge, because it was the site of many Washington suicides, and then into Adams Morgan, my old neighborhood, a renovated, groovy part of town.

The taxi dropped us off at The Ontario's first porch, with its two ionic white pillars. Stanley, the African operator, now grey-haired, remembered me and buzzed us in. We walked down the long hallway to Apartment 107. Using the brass knocker in the shape of a fist, which my mother had moved from Apartment 105 to her new dwelling, I banged on the door. She opened the heavy front door dressed in tailored pants and a silk blouse. Her eyes, large, grey-blue like my own, looked clear and bright. As she hugged me, I didn't smell the usual alcohol breath, and I exhaled a sigh of relief. She then hugged Sarah, in an unusual display of informality. My mother was well-practiced at shaking hands, but she wasn't really a hugger. She either liked you or disliked you—there was no in-between. If she disliked you, her sarcasm and dirty looks could be ferocious. I took another deep breath.

In the living room, my mother had a large brass cage, where she kept her blue macaw, who she named Wolfie. She had remodeled the kitchen, black lacquer modern efficiency style, and the bathroom, adding a teakwood Jacuzzi. It looked and felt like a gay bachelor's pad, not the start-over home of a middle-aged working woman with three young adult children who had left home.

She offered us her bedroom. She would sleep on the living room couch, a new, boxy, white upholstered couch that bore no resemblance to the old yellow couch. I protested. She insisted.

My mother took us out for a late dinner. We walked a few blocks through a changed neighborhood. Adams Morgan was now up and coming. The Spanish-fried churros hole-in-the-wall was gone. The 8-track and incense storefront had moved. Our destination, La Fourchette, was a French bistro with a large Toulouse-Lautrec mural on its wall. They served a wonderful, authentic bouillabaisse.

We sat down at a table covered with a white tablecloth. My mother skipped her usual vodka tonics and ordered a bottle of red wine. I was happy about my mother's self-imposed moderation. Maybe she had turned a corner and didn't need vodka all the time to numb out.

"Did she really mean to kill herself in the gas oven?" Sarah asked my mother about her college roommate, Sylvia Plath.

"Sylvia could be quite hysterical. I don't think she meant to kill herself. She was crying for help. There were too many people who were supposed to come to her rescue. The babysitter was late. The neighbor upstairs should have smelled the gas. A friend was meant to drop by. Sometimes she did really stupid things to get attention," my mother concluded.

Suicide was the ultimate pain you could inflict on someone. When my mother threatened to kill herself, my sister and I felt we had to comply with her every whim. Sylvia wanted people to pay attention to her pain. My mother was the same. She also wanted attention.

"You know, Sylvia and I peeled potatoes together in the school cafeteria. We both had to have jobs to pay for books. The scholarships weren't enough, and our mothers struggled financially—no fathers. We both lost our fathers when we were seven years old. Nasty job we had. I brought my own sharpened potato peeler—made the job much easier," my mother told us.

"Sylvia was so much wilder than me. She climbed out our dorm window after curfew and met up with college guys who had cars. They drove up from Yale and as far as Princeton," she said, "I couldn't do that sort of thing."

My mother was more naïve. Her first marriage was annulled when she discovered her husband was gay. Sylvia wrote in her journal about my mother's creepy courtship. Sylvia was a strong woman, so was my mother, and both had been miserable in their marriages. Both had been ambitious and wanted a career and to raise a family. Both had succeeded at their careers but failed in their personal lives.

Most of the women of my mother and Sylvia's generation and from their economic background had raised their families and never considered a career. Betty Friedan warned about the consequences, "the problem that has no name," a form of suburban depression that many women who raised children and did not work outside their homes experienced. At their commencement address in 1955, Governor Adlai Stevenson told the all-female graduates of Smith College, "… as wives and mothers … [what] you have learned and can learn will fit you for the primary task of making homes and whole human beings …" My mother and Sylvia balked at this limited role in society, but there were insurmountable pressures to conform. Most of the advertisements at that time showed the woman in the home or as a sex object draped over a luxury car. Sexism was the norm.

In Plath's journals she wrote, "… hear me, take me to your heart, be warm and let me cry and cry and cry. And help me be strong: oh [Sarah] …" It was not easy for them, with virtually no role models, but they loved each other as college roommates.

"How did you get the job at the Federal Reserve Board?" my new lover Sarah probed, while dipping her French bread in the fish stew.

"The Human Resource manager asked me to put University of Mississippi, Oxford on the government application, not the distinguished Oxford College in England." My mother enjoyed the reminiscing.

"What, were they nuts?"

My mother laughed. She didn't have her usual chip-on-the-shoulder grudge about how life had treated her. Maybe she could better accept her circumstances. My mother was sticking to two glasses of wine and didn't order another bottle. I felt relieved.

"My mother was an art teacher and, when she got pregnant with me, she quit her job. I was the oldest daughter. She was frustrated at home with four girls. Her diversion was to get together with the other moms at Girl Scouts and go camping together. She taught art on the weekends. But she didn't have a career. During World War II, my mother attended Carnegie Institute of Technology because most of the men were fighting overseas. My mother was talented and in the same class as Andy Warhol. They both started out as window dressers, but my mother quit to raise a family," said Sarah.

"Yes, it was unusual for women to become artists, at that time," my mother said.

"Mom, we're going to shoot *Big Red* in an old London church," I said. "We made arrangements to take the sets on the QE2 to England, thanks to Cliff the Third, your classmate at Oxford who's a part owner of Cunard Line. And Joseph Papp is backing us with a grant from the N.E.A. and producing our puppet animation film, so it'll get easier financially."

"Well, Cliff's one of those racing yacht types—reminds me of the guy I met last weekend at a French restaurant on Connecticut Avenue. He told me he was in town to testify before the Senate Finance Committee on "most-favored-nation status for Romania, another one of those East bloc countries trying to get support from the West. Claimed he taught philosophy, had trading companies in N.Y.C., Geneva, and Vienna. He offered to put me up for free, any-time I came to N.Y.C., at his rented suite at the Waldorf-Astoria Hotel or, if I preferred, he'd send a car to take me to his estate with a swimming pool in Spring Valley. These men seem to be very quick at sorting through one's assets and liabilities. I can see the problem of a woman in the 19th century being forced to marry for convenience."

"Mom, you wouldn't do that, would you? Marry for the money?" I asked.

"It could be easier than being on my own—especially at my age."

We promised to pay her back as soon as the grant came in from the National Endowment for the Arts. She didn't scold me for using her credit card. My mother was supportive, proud, and interested in our work. She liked Sarah. It was a turning point with my mother. I was no longer the confrontational young adult. Sarah fostered a healthy mother-daughter relationship between us. New paths were forging.

Sarah liked my mother and admired her achievements. I had the desire for recognition for my work, which was not that different from my mother's and Sylvia's desires. I never had suicidal thoughts, but I did go into dangerous situations, war zones, where I could have been killed. Strange how mothers and daughters bound together and repeated the same patterns. At the time, I was totally unconscious of the similarities.

Exploring new frontiers of sexuality was my razor's edge. I had the haughtiness, righteousness, and entitlement of a woman of a new generation. I thought I had all the answers. I did not live during a time when restraints and limitations were culturally enforced. No, I believed I could do whatever I wanted, have sex with whomever I wanted, and be free to choose my profession.

Sarah and I were discreet in D.C. We didn't talk about what had happened on the train, but once we returned to New York and the sixth floor loft, we headed straight to the bedroom. We climbed the ladder to the queen size bed, high off the ground. Sarah's weight pressed me down on the foam mattress. Long kisses. Hips dancing. Then the taste—salty, warm, twinge of metallic, sharp flavor. There was an opening, oneness, deep spasms, and letting go into the soft, fleshy tongue of another woman.

My identity was redefined through a sexual act. My mind expanded to encompass who I was becoming, over the weeks after I first made love to a woman. There was the pleasure of touching her soft curves, connecting with the feminine through a sexual act, becoming more intimate, going deeper. Then there were the labels, lesbian or bisexual. They felt too bland, too limiting, too confusing. Sarah and I were more than these labels and the sex they represented. We were partners to make the world a better place. And then there was George. I wasn't ready to let him go. I loved them both. I had to let go of old ideas of social judgments and transcend them, to live the authentic experience, to love a woman and a man at the same time.

My mother's name was Sarah. My father's name was George: the names of my two lovers. Some kind of synchronicity or message? I believed my parents reflected my significant others in name only. Not really.

George accepted this polyamorous situation. His goal was to finish the Navy and move to New York. He didn't want to lose me.

*   *   *

Nine months later, I called my father, "Dad, George is coming to New York. He's finished his military service. Could you bring his sound equipment? It would mean a lot, if he had his turntable and speakers." My father was storing the stereo that George had left when he last visited me. Over the past two years, I had traveled to different ports to meet my sailor, while he served on a Greek naval ship. One port George sailed into was Boston, where he met my father. Another port was Baltimore, where he met my mother.

"I've been reading Epicurus, a Greek philosopher who had a way to attain a happy, tranquil life. Peace and freedom from fear and pain. George will know all about it," my father said.

"Not sure about that. But are you coming to New York for business anytime soon?" I asked.

My father brought George's things the next time he was in New York. He stayed at the St. Regis, now that his business was taking off. A night at the hotel was more than a month's rent for me. George and I went to see him for breakfast in his suite.

"How're you getting on here in New York?" my father asked George.

"It's hard to find a more permanent place we can rent. Everything is overpriced," George replied.

"Yeah, we've been subletting friends' places over the last three months, moving each month, uptown, downtown, even stayed in Jersey City," I said.

"How's the work with Sarah and *Big Red*?" my father asked me.

"That's a struggle too, hard to get funding. I've been writing a lot of grant proposals but nothing's coming through," I said. "Reagan cancelled our N.E.A. grant from Joseph Papp. N.E.A.'s budget was slashed. We were nearly stranded in England, after we took the *Big Red* sets on the QE2 and our funding fell through."

I kept most of the intimate parts of my life a secret from my father. I didn't tell him about my special arrangement with George and Sarah, our unorthodox living arrangements. I was more comfortable listening to my father philosophize about life, catching up on his latest business ventures, and checking in on his latest retreats at the Zen Monastery, where he was dedicating more and more of his time.

When George and I were living together, I felt like a kid whose parents had joint custody, alternating weekends. I was sleeping at the loft with Sarah three nights and with George four nights.

George wanted reassurance from me that I loved him, that I wanted to be with him. Sex connected me to George and to Sarah. We never tried a threesome. Each partner satisfied a craving in me. I stayed attached to these relationships from a desperate need to feel loved.

Since Joseph Papp's N.E.A. grant didn't work out, Sarah and I worked together on making films with hospitalized children, funded by New York State, which paid the bills while we continued fundraising for *Big Red*. Our major obstacle was the fact that we wanted to make a puppet film with a political theme. The Muppets were the only puppets people knew about in the movies, and we had to keep explaining that Sarah's puppets were different. The puppets in *Big Red* made the film whimsical and hard for the mainstream and the art world to grasp.

Epicurus's ideals of pursuing pleasure had turned into pain, confusion, anger, and fear in my life. All I could see was my love, stretched by the hours, moving between lovers, turning me into a micromanager of my work, my relationships, and the future.

In February, George and I were staying at Hotel 17, on 17th Street between Third Avenue and Second, one of the cheapest hotels in New York City. George was acting like a divorced husband, having trouble getting on his feet. He had a six-month visa, no green card, and so work was limited, unless we married. He was a trained audio engineer who had mixed sound for Blondie and Emmylou Harris. Plus, he had been the camera person and sound person on the BBC Afghanistan documentary he shot with John. His résumé was good. George and I walked through the Hotel 17 lobby. The 60-watt light fixture was so dusty it was more like a 40-watt bulb. The fifty-year-old, crew cut receptionist wore a grayed t-shirt, smoked, and didn't look up when we passed him and entered the elevator. I plopped down on the worn, pink bedspread in Room 201. The same dirty 60-watt light fixture hid the grunge in the room. I didn't see any of our neighbors, only heard footsteps outside the door going to the bathroom down the hall or to the elevator across the hall, its squeaky door opening and closing.

"This is the pits," I told George, when we woke up.

"Sweetie, we'll be OK," he said.

"You don't remember the last place in Jersey City. Cockroaches so big, we could hear them running across the floor. The all-night boom boxes outside the bedroom window. Hotel 17 is worse. Remember what happened last night?" I said.

"You wanted to be back in Manhattan."

"Yes, but not this."

The previous night, a couple on the other side of the bedroom wall had started shouting at 3 a.m. She screamed, he threw things, glasses crashed.

"Mother Fucker ... Cunt ... Fuck off!" he yelled.

"Should we call the police?" George had asked.

"Not sure. Maybe check with the receptionist downstairs," I said.

George put on his jeans and white T-shirt, unlocked the door, and took the elevator to the lobby. I locked the door, nauseous and craving Sarah's loft bed. There were soft knocks, I opened the door. George climbed back in bed with me.

We listened to loud knocks next door, "Man, quiet down in there. You're disturbing our guests," the receptionist said.

"Fuck off," the man said.

"I'll call the police if I get another complaint."

Peace was restored. But how did I get here? I had navigated a complex, intertwining, open relationship with Sarah and George. I shared the inner explorations of self, my sexual passions, my work, my dreams. It was a demand I placed on my lovers, a sense of entitlement and desire to stay together. The roles changed and adapted from lovers to friends to partners back to lovers. I was causing pain to the two people I loved the most. They had my parents' names, George and Sarah, and they shared their absolute love for me, which healed deep wounds and childhood scars, while I inflicted suffering on them. I observed the tangled emotions I provoked and my reactions. Neither Sarah nor George confronted me. They let me move between them without a fight or even a disagreement. When I returned, I saw a despondency, a sadness, especially in George. Sarah became more anxious to get more proposals out, to work harder, and to find a way to make *Big Red*. The stress pushed Sarah and me to distance ourselves as lovers.

I saw myself lose myself, mostly reacting to the situation I had created years ago. I wanted this arrangement. Now that I had it, it was not working.

Sarah was admirably patient with my comings and goings, waiting for the situation to sort itself out. Her strength to endure was in equal proportion to my selfish tenacity to keep trying, even in the face of defeat.

* * *

In March of 1985, after Gorbachev was elected, President Reagan took a hard line against the Soviet Union. His administration openly provided military support to anti-communist armed movements in Afghanistan, Angola, and Nicaragua. Reagan also ordered an enormous peacetime defense build up. Reagan's propaganda heated up the fear and anger between the U.S. and Communist countries. He wanted Americans to hate the Russians and sent political messages about the escalation of nuclear arms and the possibility of nuclear war. American citizens were pushing back with grassroots efforts to form sister cities between cities in the U.S. and Soviet Union.

At the loft, Patricia was telling us how she would be traveling to the Soviet Union with a group of American teenagers, a peace mission. George sat next to me at the kitchen table, Sarah across from me. We knew Patricia from an exchange of business cards at a grassroots event for better relations between the U.S. and the Soviet Union.

"Would you want to make a documentary about our trip to Moscow with the Visions of Peace teenagers?" Patricia asked. "We want Americans to see that the people there are like us, not the monsters they are portrayed as in the news."

Her dark curls and brown eyes were beautiful. She had an organization called "Visions of Peace," which we believed in, and could raise the needed money for the film.

Here was some good news. This film project could be our salvation, pull us all together, get us out of the rut we were in, give *Big Red* a rest, and further our cause of improving relationships with the U.S.S.R.

George and I had been living at Hotel 17 for a couple of weeks, and I was staying there less and less, preferring the loft. However, I slept on the single bed by the window, and Sarah climbed up to her queen bed at night. I wanted some space.

The kitchen window was open, and the sticky flypaper covered with dead black flies waved in the cool breeze. I hoped Patricia didn't notice the disgusting ribbon. One of the loft roommates had put it up.

"I could probably get CBS to loan us a video camera," I said. "Sarah could direct and George could be the sound person." George was silent, while I laid out the roles.

"We have contacts at the Soviet embassy for the visa," Sarah said, "but it could be really difficult. The last news crew, the first to get permission to shoot in years, was thrown out for an interview they did with the KGB."

"Can you really pay for all our travel and production expenses?" I asked, more concerned about the money.

Patricia said she could raise the necessary funds. Later, we found out she was dating a rich guy, a Wall Street stock broker type. He became our anonymous donor.

I would be traveling again. It had been over a year since I returned from Afghanistan. All the researching, proposal writing, networking, and fundraising were a big energy and time drain. There was not much to show for all the work, and we were broke. This documentary would make me a filmmaker again. Carrying a camera, shooting in new locations, editing—the whole process would be a thrill. And the story would be a first: American teenagers traveling to the Soviet Union to meet their counterparts. What's more, there had been no American documentary about anything to do with the Soviet Union for over five years.

The more we researched about going to the Soviet Union, the more incredulous people were about our prospects of getting permission to film there. Former State Department experts, professors of Soviet studies, and grassroots organizers could not imagine that we had a chance of entering into the country with a film crew.

But CBS was interested. My experience in Afghanistan proved to be my calling card, and they agreed to loan us the camera equipment and give us some upfront money for expenses, in exchange for first refusal rights. I was also able to get several grants, including a donation from the Rockefeller Foundation, and some smaller grants from leftist organizations for salaries.

Sarah and I proceeded as if everything would work out, but we were not sure about the visa. Sarah made the formal request for the visa and location permits to the Soviet Embassy through her Soviet contacts. We hoped for the best.

George's six-month visa had two months left on it. He would be given six more months when he came back from the Soviet Union. But I couldn't do it. I couldn't take him to the Soviet Union. The thought of him near me constantly made me want to scream.

I changed my mind and gave his sound job to Margaret. She was part of our *Big Red* team, helped write grants, build sets, etc. Margaret had an Ivy League pedigree, was an excellent script editor, and had major family connections in the Washington, D.C. political arena. However, she was totally unqualified as an audio person. George agreed to train her—how to hold a boom in front of an interviewee, how to set the audio tone on the tapes before recording, how to listen to the levels and ride them, and what kinds of mics to use for the different situations. He seemed relieved to train, to be left behind, and not be part of the women-only crew. Margaret looked blasé when George explained the technical details about sound recording. She was more of a literary type and had never shown any interest in shooting or audio before. I suspected Margaret was much more interested in going to the Soviet Union than learning the technical skills we were counting on.

We also hired Jennifer, a woman in her mid-thirties, to be our Russian interpreter. She came highly recommended from one of Margaret's political contacts in D.C., who had told us Jennifer was dating a famous underground musician in Leningrad. We had met Jennifer for coffee just once. Her initial fresh-off-the-farm mid-Western look and long, flaming red hair did not prepare us for her otherwise no-nonsense attitude. She let it slip that her frequent trips into the Soviet Union made her suspect with Soviet authorities. However, we had no time to find someone else.

While we waited for the visa, I had crippled my man and, at the same time, wouldn't let him go. George wasn't making any friends. He slept long hours when I wasn't around; he depended on me for all his emotional needs. His only desire was to marry me. Could I live with a man who only wanted to care for me? The idea made me cringe. My parents' disastrous marriage haunted me.

I called both my parents to tell them I was hoping to make a documentary in the Soviet Union. And, just in time, the telegram arrived at the loft from the Soviet government simply stating: "BIG RED CAN COME."

CHAPTER 8

BEHIND THE IRON CURTAIN

After I picked up my luggage at the Sheremteyevo Airport in Moscow, I tentatively approached one of the long tables lined up in a row, where green uniformed guards wore captain-style hats with the Soviet red star pin centered over their foreheads. They dutifully examined every item brought into the Soviet Union. I had packed ballpoint pens as gifts. Jennifer, our translator, said they would be appreciated here. Otherwise, my personal items were few: several pairs of corduroys (no jeans because I heard that people from the black market would ask to buy them off of me on the street, and I didn't want the hassle), a few flannel plaid shirts, and a rust-colored down vest. We also brought CBS's Sony Betacam video camera, a Nikon still camera, twenty rolls of 35mm film, two microphones, 10 hours of Betacam tapes, a small monitor, a boom, cables, batteries, a recharger, three portable lights, light stands, a large tripod, and a transformer.

Jennifer had warned me about making sure to have the video camera, blank tapes, and other equipment listed on my passport, so I could bring them back out of the country. She also advised me to handle the camera on my own.

Jennifer had been right. The customs official fulfilled my request to list my video camera on my passport, communicating in fluent English, and with an accommodating attitude. After exiting the customs hall, I looked around for our small film crew. I spotted Jennifer's long red hair across the room immediately, then next to her saw Sarah and Margaret. Then, I searched around for the Visions of Peace leaders, Patricia and Martha. They were busy chaperoning the teenagers. Martha, dressed like a school teacher with stockings, a sensible length skirt, and short pumps, was constantly doing a head count so no one went missing. Patricia smiled, her red lipstick in perfect condition after the fourteen- hour-journey from New York to Helsinki to Moscow. We gathered outside in the arrivals hall, where a large poster of Lenin towered over us. We were in the Soviet Union, the forbidden country, the Evil Empire.

Natasha, our very own guide appointed by the Soviet government, easily spotted us—a six-woman collective with fifteen teenagers in tow on the trip of a lifetime. Her thick framed glasses and brown hair in a bun gave her an authoritarian air. Her heels clacked on the cement floor as she approached us. Her right arm extended to shake each of our hands several feet before we could reach her. She was brisk and business-like, huddling us all together into a compact group to usher us on to the blue-striped, state bus waiting outside.

"Come, come," she said in English, with a heavy Russian accent.

Jennifer immediately suspected Natasha was a spy. She had advised us before we left New York that we would have to be careful about what we said once we were in the Soviet Union. The authorities would keep a watchful eye on us at all times, she told us. We could expect video cameras in our hotel rooms.

Sarah and I thought this was pure American paranoia. After all, the authorities had granted us permission to film. And Natasha was probably here to help us. We would be shooting a documentary about American teenagers meeting their Soviet counterparts in Moscow, Tbilisi, Yerevan, and Leningrad. We had twelve days to shoot everything. Both our group and project were called "Visions of Peace." We were certainly not after state secrets. We wanted to find teenagers hanging out who could talk to our kids and do what teenagers do all over the world, dance at a disco, drink sodas together, cheer at sports events. We would shoot these casual encounters and show Americans that Soviets were not so different from us.

On the state bus leaving Moscow airport, I was holding the 22 lb. Betacam shooting the grey cement apartment buildings in the rain. Sarah tapped me on the shoulder and directed me to shoot the kids sitting two-by-two in rows. Margaret pointed the mic on a boom over our heads. Clare, a Quaker, 14 years old with dimpled, freckled cheeks, smiled and then turned to look out the window. Sitting next to her was Harold, a gangly, tall African American boy from Harlem. He passed a music cassette to Stephen, who sat across the aisle. Stephen was the oldest teenager, a 15-year-old Jewish boy from Long Island. Jennifer dozed off. Her head leaned against the fogged window. Next to Jennifer, Natasha watched us from her aisle seat. The other kids giggled and chatted or napped for the half hour ride to the hotel. On the bus ride, Patricia was hyped up. Her dream was coming true: Americans meeting Soviets. Her eyes were wide like a beauty queen on the town parade float, as we rode into Moscow.

It was late spring in Moscow, but it felt like winter. The rain had turned to icy sheets. We checked into a high-rise modern hotel on the outskirts of the capital. We turned in our passports to the hotel clerks and dropped off our bags in our rooms. The group paired off. Sarah and I shared a room. Margaret roomed with Jennifer. Natasha lived in a state-assigned communal flat nearby.

We had three to four days in each city, and Sarah wanted to start right away. So, we decided to meet in the hotel lobby and take the subway to Red Square without delay. Margaret brought the bulky wooden tripod. I held the video camera on my shoulder. Sarah carried the camera bag with the Betacam tapes. We walked outside into the icy rain and down into the metro station in the square in front of the hotel. Down the long escalator and into the depth of the underground, chandeliers glistened and reflected on the polished white and black checkered marble floors. A silent, silver train glided into a vast ballroom-like space to take us to our destination, the Ploshchad Revolyutsii station on the Green line. The hushed voices and glamour of the Moscow metro were nothing like the bowels of New York's subway system that smelled of urine and was filled with graffitied, rattling subway trains and the masses shouting, hawking candy bars, begging for change.

I didn't expect the public services in a communist country to be so ornate. We were in the heart of Mother Russia, Tolstoy's Moscow, where tragedies happened in opulent homes, where Sarah's glamorized *Big Red* puppets wanted to make friends with an American woman. I had seen the Soviet dark side, the murderous side, the invasion in Afghanistan, but I had softened from Sarah's influence. I joined a tribe of women that celebrated feminine ways, Visions of Peace—nurturing through relationships, truth at a grassroots level, independent media, making a documentary for a social cause, and the prospect of better understanding between people from opposing nations.

On the color TV in the lobby of our Moscow hotel, the Soviet news was broadcasting Gorbachev, the recently elected General Secretary, giving a speech about the upcoming 40th Anniversary of the Great Victory of the Great Patriotic War. There would be a parade on Victory Day in several weeks, on May 9th. Perestroika and glasnost were gaining ground, which promised less censorship and corruption. However, it would be years before there was major cooperation between our two governments.

Our group toured Red Square like tourists. Huge posters with Soviet insignias hung everywhere, the hammer and sickle, Lenin's face peering out of the red banner, Cyrillic phrases in black lettering, all special decorations for the upcoming 40th year anniversary. Tanks were parked on the squares for display, just like the ones I saw in Afghanistan. Red and yellow flags flew above the cement walls. I could hear, in my mind, the Soviet military band playing, as I remembered the black and white footage I saw in the hotel lobby commemorating the defeat of the Nazis in 1945. The TV showed thousands of soldiers in dress uniforms, adorned in parade brocade and belts, marching through this square forty years ago. Soviet generals, with rows of medals pinned to their uniforms, made speeches. Then, they focused on large, red-tipped, grey missiles attached to

Soviet trucks getting ready for the upcoming public showing. Natasha took us to Lenin's statue, a man in a black trench coat, encased in metal. I filmed the kids looking up at the image of Lenin, four stories tall, draped on the back wall of Red Square. Young cadets with bayonets kicked their black boots high in a goose stepping march. The Soviet Red Square and monuments dwarfed the Russian Orthodox church and its multiple gold domes.

"What do you think about the defeat of the Nazis?" Sarah asked Stephen, the Jewish boy from New York.

"I've heard all this before. I'm not impressed. My parents say I should care, but I don't," Stephen spoke to the camera on the large wooden tripod. Passersby stopped to watch us—a WWII vet in a wrinkled uniform with a half-arm sleeve pinned to his chest, a kerchiefed babushka lady in black boots, a younger worker wearing a 1980 Olympic T-shirt, with the cute bear emblem under an unzipped brown jacket.

Our kids were bored, jet lagged, and hungry. We returned to the hotel, where the clips from Victory Day were still playing in the lobby. Naval officers marched by with frozen faces, staring at the camera. We headed for the hotel's spacious restaurant that could seat 200 people. We ordered bottled water, already forewarned not to drink the tap water or use it to brush our teeth. Then we looked at the menu in anticipation. At ten pages long, it listed dishes in Cyrillic Russian, English, French, Spanish, and German.

Clare, the Quaker girl with freckles, asked for Chicken Kiev and orange juice in Russian. She had memorized a few phrases from a Russian-English dictionary she carried with her. The waiter looked over the long menu. Clare turned the page to the items she wanted and pointed.

"Nyet," said the waiter.

Harold, the African American boy, waved to get the waiter's attention, "I would like the meatballs and a Coke."

The waiter shook his head.

Sarah cleared her throat and asked for the Borscht and blinis.

Each item picked was not available. Jennifer jumped in and asked the waiter what they were serving, "Beef stroganoff," he replied. We all ate beef stroganoff with pickled cabbage for lunch and drank bottled water.

The next day, we boarded the state bus to visit an elementary school. We drove past the same grey cement, eight-story apartment buildings we had seen on the way in from the airport. It was another cold, rainy day, and there was no horizon. A wall of grey clouds pressed down on us. When we arrived at the school, Natasha gathered us into a tight group. I stepped ten paces behind our group to film. Margaret stood close to me to record the sound. We were attached by an eight foot wire. Natasha motioned for us to come back. I ignored her. She let us shoot. Stephen, the languid New Yorker, carried the tripod into the building.

Three well-dressed officials of the school, two women and one man, all in their forties, greeted our group and brought us into the assembly hall. The young Soviet children sat in rows of wooden chairs, straight backed, quiet, staring at the stage. A row of empty chairs in the front row faced the stage.

We all sat in the front row as Natasha climbed the stairs to the stage. The male headmaster, well-shaven, in a thick tweed suit, a red sickle and star button on his lapel, told the story about World War II in a flat voice. Natasha translated the speech sentence by tedious sentence, about how hard they fought in the war, the strength of their nation, communism, and the promise of the next generation of Soviet workers—heroic, industrious, and patriotic. After a few minutes of this rhetoric, I turned off the camera, now resting on the tripod in front of me. The national pride derived from fighting the Germans in World War II, defeating Nazism, and establishing a communist government would not work in our documentary and would not change the way Americans thought about the Soviet Union one bit.

The next day, Natasha loaded us on the same bus and took us to GUM, the state department store, near Red Square. The light sparkled through the vast glass-paned roof, where boutique shops lined two floors. Garish necklaces hung on the walls in one empty store. A long line flowed from another store, where we heard they recently procured a shipment of bathing suits from France. This large mall was the only place stocked with Western goods. Most of the items were too expensive for Muscovites.

Back at the hotel, Sarah and I reviewed the footage we had shot in the last three days. We were disappointed with the forty minutes we had. The content so far was mostly propaganda and would work against our message. There were technical problems. I looked at the blurry shots shifting in and out of focus, like they were shot on a home movie camera with the automatic focus used by amateurs. I couldn't figure out how to turn off this feature. Ugh. This couldn't be happening.

Sarah and I went to find Jennifer to ask about our locations. I knocked on her hotel door. She cracked the door, peered out, and looked in both directions for clear passage. She put on her coat and took us out the back hotel staircase and onto the street.

"Jennifer, I'm concerned about our guide, Natasha. She is taking us to tourist sites and to schools where they only give speeches," I said.

Jennifer told me to hush and kept walking five blocks away from the hotel until we were on a street with the cement apartment buildings behind us. Now it was safe to discuss the matter.

"We want places where teenagers hang out, local eating places, discos, soccer matches, someone's home. We'll make a list," Sarah said.

"You don't understand. This is the Soviet Union not Kansas," Jennifer said. "They don't want ordinary people talking to foreigners. People disappear here for the tiniest of infractions."

"What can we do?" I asked.

"Maybe Tbilisi will be better. I'm making no promises."

Maybe I needed to talk to Natasha directly. At least she wouldn't insist on meeting us on the street, in the cold night, to discuss the itinerary.

* * *

At 2 a.m., Natasha met us in the hotel lobby with the same formality she had used on the first day and told us she would not accompany us. We would have a new guide, when we arrived in the capital of Georgia.

We boarded the familiar bus and headed to the Moscow airport for our flight to Tbilisi, Georgia. We were the only foreigners at the Moscow airport, waiting in the open space for the flight to board. Domestic flights took place in the middle of the night. Jennifer told us this was so that no one could see or sneak aerial pictures of regional airports. Another poster of Lenin greeted us on the wall. An old man with a wrinkled jacket buttoned up to the collar, ten medals pinned to the right side of his chest, put a few kopeks into a metal vending machine. A bottle of vodka dispensed out of the machine. He drank its content in one long gulp standing. His large nose turned red as I stared.

"Zdravstvuyte tovarisch," blasted from the TV, the familiar phrase, "Hello comrade," narrated over more archived parade footage rolling by. Natasha waved goodbye to us on the runway. A few officials with flashlights guided us on this starless night, as we climbed the stairs up to the small plane.

On the Aeroflot flight, there was nothing to see but darkness out of the tiny windows. No refreshments were served. We flew south. A few Soviet businessmen and a giggly group of American teenagers traveled together.

"What's so funny?" I asked the kids.

"Clare stole a roll of Soviet toilet paper from the hotel," Harold told me. He had been shy about speaking up in the past.

"Whatever for?" I asked.

"Nobody would believe this stuff. It's so rough and crappy. Probably clog our toilets back home," Clare told me.

"I hope you don't get shipped off to Siberia for lifting TP," I joked.

* * *

It was Day 4 when we arrived in Tbilisi. After less than three hours of sleep, I felt refreshed and happy for the change to this more Mediterranean-like, sunny city. We sat in the dining room looking out at the hotel garden. The breakfast buffet had strawberries, yogurt, and fresh baked bread that looked like Afghani bread.

Gregory, a well-tanned man with a large mustache, hurried into the hotel to meet us after breakfast. He was our new guide and translator.

His warm, lingering handshake promised a more fun time here. He sat with Sarah and me, crossed his legs, and smoked Zolotoye Runo brand cigarettes in a relaxed and open manner. We couldn't find a trace of the Soviet uptightness we were used to. Clare came over to further discuss a plan she and Sarah had talked about on the plane. The rest of the group was sprawled at the different tables, lingering before the next marching orders. Jennifer slept late and missed breakfast.

Clare, a 14-year-old peace activist, had marched in D.C. with her Quaker parents, where she handed out anti-war leaflets and wore a cardboard sign, "No More Nuclear Missiles." She brought clown makeup and wanted to wear it.

"I like the idea. Yes, let's find a way to use it today," Sarah said.

Gregory nodded, "We'll go to an art school today," he said in fluent English, with only a hint of an accent I didn't recognize.

Inwardly, I moaned. I still wanted us to film teenagers in more natural settings.

"This'll work," said Sarah, before I could make a different request.

Later, Clare flitted from table to table, recruiting kids to go with her to the hotel room and paint their faces white, make their lips bright red, and line their eyes in black. All the kids agreed except Stephen, who didn't want to participate.

He came over to sit with us, while the rest bounded into the hotel.

"What do you think of this new idea?" I asked. "Could be fun."

"It's a stupid idea. We're like the only Americans here, and we're going to look like clowns. No way am I going to do that," Stephen said.

Clare skipped into the lobby with her clown face, and the rest of the kids following her with their circus makeup.

"You look good," said Gregory, when he saw Clare beaming in her make-up.

The bus pulled up, and we all climbed aboard for another Soviet school experience. Margaret sat in the back of the bus with the kids, the rest of the adults sat in the front.

At the assembly, in a large room, the principal, a middle-aged woman in a floral dress, stood on the side. The kids, kindergarteners to third graders, were seated in small groups singing songs, playing simple clapping games, chatting casually. Clare, with her mime troupe, wove through the seated children. Then, she took the hand of one of the littlest kids. She picked a cherub-faced, dark- haired, six-year-old girl, with two braids pinned on the top of her head. She pulled her on the stage, and they both sat down, cross legged, facing each other. At eye level, Clare put her grimaced face inches away from the girl's nose. The little girl saw a boogie man. Her eyes grew big, she exhaled, she tensed, her eyes filled with tears. A single tear fell down her cheek. I was filming close, and recorded Clare's made-up face on Betacam tape. Clare moved away before she saw the young girl's teardrop.

A first grader, with a red scarf tied around her neck, ran away to hide behind her teacher when Clare approached. Clare grew fierce, stone-faced, the painted smile fixed on her face. She was mad that this girl didn't want to participate. After that, Clare stood far away from all the children, leaning against the wall, waiting for the event to be over.

Harold, the Harlem kid, had the biggest grin. He spun around in a circle and moonwalked, Michael Jackson-like, over to the third graders. He became the Pied Piper, as the rest of class followed him clapping, dancing, and celebrating.

A little ballerina dressed in white stockings and ballet slippers performed a solo dance, twirling, moving faster and faster as she cantered across the stage. The Russian music matched her pace. She mesmerized us all with her grace, beauty, and elegance.

I caught each moment in short fragments, MTV style, my way of compensating for the focus problem. The shots heightened the disconnection, sped up the event. And the extreme close-ups of the children's faces, both the clown faces and the Tbilisi children, grasped an underlying intensity and tension between the Americans and Soviets.

"Clare, how is this trip for you?" Sarah asked, while Margaret held the boom mic and I filmed the interview outside the assembly room. Stephen had set up the tripod for us and looked bored during the interview. He had a crush on Margaret and wanted to be near her all the time.

"Those soldiers' goose-stepping boots, they're all Nazis. I hate them all," she answered.

Sarah and I didn't react, trying to be professionals, but this was not the answer we expected. Where did we see soldiers goose stepping? In Moscow at Red Square. Clare had put the Soviets on a pedestal, expecting them to welcome her like her Quaker community. She was disillusioned, like a scorned lover. She was angry when the little girl ran away from her.

Clare kept her makeup on for the rest of the day, while the other Visions of Peace kids washed theirs off. People on the streets stared at her. She stared back. The clown was severe, taunting, and almost aggressive.

Patricia called a meeting that night. When we gathered, the Visions of Peace clan sang "We shall overcome someday" and other peace folk songs. Margaret sat with the kids, her arm around Clare. It felt like an "us vs. them" line was being drawn. Kids were on one side, adults on the other, except Margaret, who had joined the kids on the other side. Stephen sat next to her. Martha, Patricia's partner, stood far away from both groups. Silent. Her arms were folded and her face held a disapproving look, while she watched all of us. Jennifer retired early to her hotel room. Gregory had gone home for the night.

"We felt manipulated. The clown makeup was staged, not natural. It isn't our truth," Margaret spoke as if she was one of the teenagers.

Margaret blamed the film crew for the incident in the school. It had been wrong to have the kids wear clown makeup that scared the Tbilisi children, she told everyone.

"What are you talking about? What is truth?" I answered my own questions, "What happened in the moment happened. Both the positive and negative."

"No, you made the kids into clowns, made them upset those children in that school," Margaret said.

"If you don't like what I'm doing, I'll throw my camera in the river. Sarah and I are a team. We did what we thought was best." My pent-up rage released, I realized my mistake. I was mad at Margaret for refusing to carry the tripod and hadn't said anything. There were shots we couldn't use because Stephen held a tripod in the video frame. I had left George behind to bring Margaret and regretted this decision. It felt like this meeting was a mutiny, with accusations coming from Margaret, a member of our crew.

I was so caught up in the drama, I lost all perspective. Women-fighting was happening behind the scenes. Margaret gathered support from the kids, talking to them like she was running for class president. Sarah and I didn't see it coming; we were too focused on making the documentary.

The tension and anger were still palpable when Patricia stopped the meeting, and we all went to bed. I couldn't sleep that night. My mind went over and over the day's events. The Visions of Peace group was fighting. Patricia was holding the group together as best she could. Martha had distanced herself from both groups, the teen-agers and the film crew. The teenagers also seemed divided among themselves, between the ones who thought the Soviet Union was evil and those who thought it was an amazing place. It seemed that the more disadvantaged children, like Harold, loved the experience, being treated with respect, included in all the activities, with no signs of prejudices. Stephen was the only one who didn't take a side. He couldn't care less about the politics. He had heard about the horrors of the Holocaust and World War II too many times before. "Who really cares?" he told us on camera at a cameo interview out-side the school.

Gregory returned the next morning at breakfast in the garden.

"I think a trip to the Caucasus Mountains today would be good for everyone. They are beautiful," he told us.

Sarah and I were exhausted. Sarah hadn't slept either. After a few hours lying awake, we both realized the other one wasn't asleep, and we talked for hours about the previous day's experience.

At dawn, before breakfast, we reviewed the footage on the small monitor in our hotel room. We were excited by the drama, the unfolding of the events, the contradictions, no right or wrong, just personal experiences based on individual filters, projections, back-ground. The prejudices and judgments were more about the person than the event.

The peacenik kid hated the Soviets. The ghetto kid felt like a king in the Soviet Union. The Jewish boy was apathetic. Stereotypes, contradictions, not one truth. This was what was important: showing the grey, not the black-and-white ten-second media spot summed up for the audience and neatly packaged. We needed complexities so we could ask the hard questions for ourselves. Where would I take a stand? Could there be a multitude of points of view? Especially, since it was about my country's adversarial stance against another country, I wanted to show how important it was to look beyond the surface, to discover humanity and the possibility for good, for what was best for all, for a change that could support everyone to be kinder, gentler, and at peace.

At breakfast, Jennifer looked refreshed and offered to take the kids to the mountains, if we wanted to stay behind and rest. We were thrilled with this offer. We were excited about the direction of the film and wanted to arrange for more encounters with local people. Showing the kids hiking by themselves in the mountains was not part of our script.

"Could we scout some scenes for tonight?" I asked Gregory, happy we had one more night in Tbilisi.

"How about I meet you for lunch?" he said. His job was to stick close to the film crew so he wasn't going with the bigger group to the mountains, now that Sarah and I were staying behind with the camera equipment.

Margaret went with the kids, and I was relieved to have some time away from her. While I was shooting, she had to be a few feet from me, and this closeness, after what had happened the night before, would be grating.

At noon, Gregory arrived in a white pressed shirt, slightly open to show his hairy chest, and blue jeans. I was surprised by his hipness. We didn't ask about the jeans, but we knew he may have gotten them on the black market.

I gave him a box of pens as a gift. It felt so lame but he seemed to appreciate it. He took us to his favorite restaurant. We walked a few blocks to a grotto-like building, with curved whitewashed walls. Large wooden tables faced a big, open, wood stove where meats were grilling. The charcoal barbecue smell made my stomach growl. We were served lots of small dishes of olives, goat cheese, baba ghanoush, hummus, stuffed peppers, tomato salad, and local wine, while the kebabs cooked. They reminded me of the Greek taverna food that George and I enjoyed.

"So, what about that disco I want?" I asked Gregory between bites.

"I'm so sorry but all plans changed. You'll be leaving tonight to Leningrad. There was a flood, and so you won't be able to go to Yerevan tomorrow," he told us.

"What?" Sarah said. "We were meant to spend another night here."

"I know, but trip is canceled. You must go to Leningrad."

"Ugh," I thought. So this was another snag.

"Natasha will meet you tonight and take you to most wonderful hotel in Leningrad. Tolstoy stayed there," Gregory told us. "She can arrange for what you want when you see her."

"Sure," I said not convinced.

The meat arrived, and Sarah and I stuffed ourselves. The freshness of the ingredients and tastiness of the meat was something we hadn't found in Moscow.

"I'm so sorry you won't see the Caucasus Mountains. They are magical. Many great mystics lived up in the mountain caves. Secret Sufi schools are hidden up there, far from Soviet communism," Gregory said, proud of his Georgian heritage. "And many dervish fairy tales come from here."

"Can you tell us one?" I asked. I was surprised how open he was, so daring to talk about ideas outside of the sanctioned Soviet script. He was the first non-Russian appointed to work with us, which may have accounted for his flexibility.

"There was a Sufi prophet who told the villagers that all the water from the well will be transformed and will make everyone crazy. Only one man paid attention and filled his ceramic jars full of the original water. The next day, the water was replaced and all the villagers acted crazy except the one man who drank his stored water. When the sane man interacted with all the others they thought he was the crazy one and ostracized him. The man became so lonely that in the end he drank the new water. The villagers regarded him as the former madman who recovered."

Sarah and I gave each other a knowing look about the story Gregory told us. He didn't have the same communist loyalties that Natasha, our first guide stuck to. Fresh, crispy baklava, made with pistachios and dripping in syrup, came and glasses of water. After we ate dessert, small ceramic cups of Georgian coffee were served. Greek, Turkish, and Georgian coffee were all the same; finely ground coffee with sugar was boiled until small bubbles appeared and deflated several times by moving the copper coffee pot on and off the fire.

After I finished my cup of coffee, there was thick sediment left at the bottom of the cup. Gregory asked me if I wanted my fortune told.

"Make a wish," he said.

"I wish for harmony and peace."

I followed his instructions and flipped the cup onto its plate, turned the cup clockwise three times, and then waited. The fine coffee grounds seeped slowly under the rim of the cup.

"Your wish will be granted but not immediately. Many years must pass first," he said, reading the first gesture.

He turned the cup over and showed me the inside, where tiny markings of stars, squares, circles, and squirrelly shapes appeared in relief.

"There's a triangle there. You are in love with two people."

OK, he had our attention.

"Some break will happen. You will be friends, but a big change is coming. Some money problems in the near future. Lots of difficulties coming, but you're strong."

"Anything good there in those grinds?" I asked.

"Always. Time passes, change happens, It's about the lessons you learn. This is life. Bondage is when you don't remember you are always free. No situation cannot be endured. Our internal demons are more dangerous than anything coming from the outside. This you need to remember." Gregory was a prophet as well as our guide.

I felt a tightness in my neck. It became hard to turn my head, as his predictions sank in. The trip had been much harder than I expected. I was feeling guilty about leaving George behind, and I really didn't want any more financial hardships. I didn't feel free right, now. I couldn't access the flow I had felt in Afghanistan, when that trip got difficult. Still, I was prepared to endure whatever happened.

* * *

Natasha marched towards us as we walked into the Pulkovo Airport in Leningrad. I shook her strong handgrip, which told me who was in charge. She accompanied us on the familiar Soviet bus, the same type we had ridden in Moscow and Tblisi. Apparently, one factory made all the state buses here.

It was Day 5, the middle of the night. Our trip was moving at jet speed, and we had arrived at the last city. Leningrad was previously St. Petersburg, the former Imperialist capital of Russia, before the communists took power in 1917. We stayed at the Angleterre Hotel, where Leo Tolstoy had been a frequent guest. The grand façade and large boutique windows on the ground floor displayed well-worn antiques, memories of better times from the past. Large, dusty velvet curtains were draped over the windows, hiding any objects in the store windows. Inside the hotel lobby, the enormous crystal chandeliers flickered a jaundiced yellow light. We carried our bags up three flights of stairs. The metal-grated brass elevator was broken.

In our suite, Sarah and I fell into the bed with brocade awnings worn thin, with holes visible. There was no sexual spark between us. Somewhere along the way, we had become less lovers, more comrades on a mission. In the morning on Day 6, I looked at the once magnificent furnishings that had been beaten over time. The sofa's threadbare upholstery sorely needed replacing.

At breakfast, our whole troupe gathered in the dining room, while Natasha dictated our schedule for the next eight days. I had been wrong about having any influence on our schedule. Jennifer spoke sharply in Russian about our demands to Natasha. She raised her voice for our cause.

"Nyet," Natasha replied.

Jennifer sat down at our table, where Sarah and I dunked the ponchiki doughnuts in lukewarm grey tea. We would visit the

Hermitage museum today. We were tourists, driven from site to site, herded on and off the Soviet bus like sheep.

On Day 7, we passed a shop where I bought nesting dolls, babushka ladies in floral dresses painted in bright colors—red, blue, green, orange, purple, yellow—all with painted smiles, red lips, blue eyes, and yellow hair under their matching kerchiefs, fitting one inside the other. In the gift shop, a TV was playing that same Soviet footage for the 40th Anniversary of the Great Victory over and over, like Coca-Cola ads interrupting *Murder She Wrote*, a favorite television show back home.

On Day 8, Natasha let the kids roam the streets. Patricia told them to go explore, and we followed them with the camera. Under the Bank Bridge, which crosses the Griboedov Canal, there stood a golden-winged griffin, a monster with the head of an eagle and body of a lion. A wedding photographer took pictures, as the teenagers ambled by. A bride, dressed in a white lace gown, and a groom in a dark suit toasted, clinking glasses filled with clear vodka. According to legend, a griffin mates for life; even if a partner dies, the other continues to live alone.

On Day 9, we passed a park, where a large statue of a man- and woman-at-arms, holding a flag, towered over the wooden benches. An old lady with a green kerchief, who looked like Sarah's Tea Lady, witchy and ogre-like but sweet, threw stale bread around. Pigeons circled her, crooning their delight. Sarah's puppets were reflected in the people I saw on the streets. Art copied life, life copied art, influences were impossible to distinguish.

On Days 10 through 12, we wasted our time visiting more tourist stores, more monuments and parks. Then, Jennifer saw a café full of teenagers near our hotel. A fierce dialogue took place, and Natasha relented. Our kids wandered into a smoky, dark space with a large mercury glass mirror hung on the wall. Our teenage boys saw the sophisticated Leningrad girls and became shy, averting their eyes. One dark, short-haired Russian girl spoke a little English and started a conversation. Stephen smiled as they began to whisper. Both were self-conscious of the camera filming them. A bolder blonde girl leaning against the wall gave Harold a big smile. He walked over to talk to her. The teenagers acted like teenagers from all over the world, awkward, exploring friendships, and flirting.

On Day 13, Jennifer was sitting with us at the breakfast table of the palace-like, run-down hotel.

"Damn," said Jennifer.

"What?" I asked.

"I don't think there was any flood in Yerevan. I can't find any news about it in the Pravda newspaper. None of my friends heard about it, either. They cut our trip in the Baltic states short. Something must not have been right for them."

I hoped that Gregory wasn't in any trouble. I couldn't imagine that the Soviet government cared about fortune telling and a Sufi story. Jennifer and I differed on this matter. We never found out the real reason we skipped Yerevan or if anything had happened to Gregory.

In the afternoon, we headed to another stuffy secondary school hall. The Soviet teenagers were dressed in navy blue uniforms, jackets, pants, and red scarves for the boys and blue dresses with the same scarves for the girls. Harold stood on a high stage and looked down at the classes filling row after row of chairs in an orderly, quiet fashion. He held his shiny brass saxophone in his hands. All eyes looked up at his. He held the silence long and strong. Then he exploded into long, feverish Coltrane solos. The audience jumped, their stern postures transformed into teenage delight. Clapping between songs, their zeal was contagious. Their teachers' eyes encouraged their fun. All applauded along, whenever they couldn't contain their amazement any longer. Harold wove his sensual sounds, crossing boundaries, making connections.

Harold's breath pushed through his instrument into a crescendo, fueling the excitement of West Meets East on Common Ground. When he finished, the standing ovation didn't quit. An encore. He moonwalked across the stage, twirled his body 360 degrees, and played his final piece.

Visions of Peace cheered Harold. We applauded, the Americans and Soviets together. Patricia hugged Martha. Margaret smiled at me, while I shot the whole scene and she recorded the music and clapping. Sarah high-fived me. All grievances between the adults and kids, between different political stances, disappeared in this moment. We were ready to go home.

On the final night, our group boarded the state bus to go to a sandy beach on the Baltic Sea, near Leningrad. A bright crescent moon shone high in the blue sky, reflecting the sunlight. The kids built a bonfire, and we all gathered around the smoky, crackling fire. The gentle sea lapped the sandy shore.

Clare began to cry. "People are suppressed here, which is so obvious to see when you walk down the street and don't hear people talking or smiling. Those horrible children finally got to smile after so much effort and hard work. They're like little machines programmed to do what the state wants. They're scared little robots."

Another teenager said, "People just stare at you. You know they want to talk to you, but they're afraid to talk to you. It's so sad. You see they want to reach out but can't."

Patricia contradicted them and said, "They're so warm. They showed us so much love and put themselves at risk to welcome us and to be honest with us. I know how different our governments are, but the thing I know most is we have to survive on this earth together."

Martha, Patricia's partner at Visions of Peace, added, "We can't do it all in a two-week period. We have to start where we are, understand where we are, and understand where they are. Find ways to get to know the people. Out of that knowing each other, communicating with each other, then we can find peace."

Then Harold joined in, "We see now the job is nowhere near finished, it is only a beginning. The symbol for peace is the dove because it flies free. We take for granted as Americans how free we are. These people really care for you, put their lives on the line to treat us and take us places. I wonder if they came to the United States, would we neglect them and put them aside? We have to think about those things."

Clare said, "We can have our own peace in our own little world, but we must have it everywhere."

The sun set over the sea, the orange-yellow sunlight reflected a beam on the water. Sarah and I went on this trip to document these kids as ambassadors and discovered that they were just kids, with their own prejudices and projections. Peace and positive relations were hard at a micro level and a macro level, but we could work toward positive relations as much as possible and as best we could, in all aspects of our lives.

* * *

"Let's call the documentary *We're Not in Kansas Anymore?*" Sarah asked, when we boarded our Finnair flight to Helsinki the next day, in broad daylight, to connect to our New York flight.

"Bit long, but I love it," I said.

The desire to make the world a better place was a high ideal. But without working on my own contributions to pain, disharmony, and suffering, I recreated conflict in the microcosm. Visions of Peace had fought, like I fought within myself. Peace had to begin at the most intimate level, starting with myself. Was I at peace with myself? No. I was fragmented. I still felt I wasn't good enough, and I felt guilty for leaving George behind. *We're Not in Kansas Anymore* showed my humanity, my flaws, my desires, hopes, and wishes, but it offered no real answers.

* * *

"I'm going back to Greece, as soon as my visa runs out. I'm living at Demetre's, helping him build an art studio in Upstate New York for the next month," George said through the phone.

I had no idea where he had disappeared to and had been waiting by the phone in the loft hallway for his call.

"Who's Demetre?" I asked.

"Demetre. He's a distant cousin. An icon painter. He restores icons in Greek Orthodox churches. My parents know his parents."

"Can I see you?"

"Maybe," he said and then agreed to meet at the newsstand at the Port Authority the following Sunday morning.

* * *

Coming out of the A train, I saw George standing by the racks of magazines, sipping on a cup of coffee from a Greek diner.

"I'm sorry I'm late. The trains are so unpredictable on Sundays," I said.

He gave me a long, lingering kiss—he couldn't help himself. I knew he was mad at me, but he loved me, too.

"How've you been?" I asked.

"OK, Demetre's place is fine. I like being out in nature and working with my hands. We're framing the new building ourselves," he said.

"Oh," I said, "How about if we walk a bit?"

We walked out of the big bus terminal onto 8th Avenue, which was mostly empty. New Yorkers like to sleep in and didn't really come out until late afternoon, if at all, on Sundays.

We held hands as we walked, and I told him in detail about my trip to the Soviet Union: the difficulties we encountered; how hard it was to get any location besides the tourist sites and state schools; the fight with Margaret and the kids over the clown scene; the intense polarity in reactions, from the kids' hatred, fear, and apathy to joy; Harold's finale saxophone performance; my regret for leaving him behind; and how much I needed his expertise and closeness.

He listened to me, interested and sad. He told me how lonely he had been when I left, how he saw that he had been too passive and that he needed to make a change.

"Demetre thinks I'm crazy to put up with this situation with you and Sarah," he said. "Either you marry me and leave Sarah, or I'm going back to Greece." I could hear he was serious and had thought about this ultimatum a lot.

"I know it's been crazy. I don't know what I was thinking. It's been hard for both of us, and I made stupid choices," I said. "And I can't marry you; I can't leave Sarah. I have to finish this documentary. It's too important to me."

I saw tears fill his eyes. I started to cry, too. We stopped and held each other on the corner of 14th Street. We walked silently east, across to Union Square, where a Harlem teenager twirled on his shoulders in a breakdance move to hip-hop music blasting from a big boom box.

"You keep my stereo over at Broome Street," George said.

I knew how much his equipment meant to him. He had eaten spaghetti and soy sauce for a year to save up the money to buy all the components in London, when we were at film school together.

"OK, thank you," I replied.

We kept walking toward Hotel 17, drawn by our physical needs. George paid for a room.

We felt our relationship was over. Through tears, clinging, hard sex, over and over, we both climaxed, made love all night, wanting every last bit of life force from each other before we departed.

The next morning, George took the subway back to the Port Authority, and I walked over to Broadway. I followed the same route I had taken three years before, when I first met Sarah. But so much had changed. The Gap had replaced the fabric store. Dean and DeLuca—with its fancy pastries and pricey fresh fruits—was bright and classy. I stopped for a cappuccino. Sipping the coffee, I was in physical pain, my vagina sore from the pounding of the night before. My breath was tight, my heart ached, and my mind went over and over what had happened in the last twenty-four hours.

I trudged up the six flights. Opening the heavy metal door with the spray painted six, the lock clunked loudly as I turned the key. I dragged my body through the studio past the *Big Red* train and puppets, down the hallway, past the silent rotary dial phone, and saw Sarah's back, where she sat at the kitchen table. I sat down across from her. My back faced the World Trade Center towers in the distance.

"Where were you last night? I was worried," Sarah said.

"I said goodbye," I told her.

"You've made up your mind."

"No, George had made up his mind. He didn't want this situation anymore. And I can't marry him. I have to finish this film, get it out there in the world."

Sarah accepted me, and was always tolerant with me and my love triangle.

Our goals were the same. We were filmmakers first. I didn't want to be a wife. I wanted my freedom more.

Sarah and I had kept our affair a secret for many years. There was a stigma at that time. Lesbians were not accepted in mainstream circles. Bisexuals were even more ostracized. By not choosing to be with one gender, I was threatening to the status quo and homosexuals. There were no role models for bisexual women in the 80s. And I wanted to fit in to succeed.

Now, I wasn't sure how to define our relationship. We were no longer sleeping together but spent all our time together.

* * *

On September 26th, 1985, Broome Street store owners and loft tenants taped large Xs on their building windows. TV news reporters claimed that masking tape would save us from imploding glass when Hurricane Gloria hit New York City the next day. Sarah had stocked up on canned food, flashlights, extra batteries, and bottled water, as instructed by the emergency announcements interrupting regular TV programming. She had also taped Xs on all our loft windows. It was going to be the biggest disaster New York had ever seen, claimed the TV journalists. I didn't care.

For several months I had been waitressing at Rozinante, a local burger joint surrounded by Soho new cuisine restaurants. Sarah had a regular table, next to the large glass window, where I served her discounted burgers and Coke, one of the perks of being a waitress. Sarah shuffled a stack of index cards, each card detailed a scene we shot in the Soviet Union. I trudged from Sarah's table, where we were paper editing *We're Not in Kansas Anymore*, to the customers' tables to take their orders, to the smoking beef burger and French fry-smelling kitchen, to the bar where Tony the bartender mixed Manhattans for the Italian-American business men, back to the kitchen where dirty dishes were piled up for the dishwasher. Each step reminded me that I was paying the rent from tips; our documentary had no more funding. I was also growing fatter by the day on the diet of free medium-rare cheeseburgers and French fries.

* * *

My mother was sending me gifts out of the blue: a black linen suit, an Irish purple wool cape, a brown leather Coach bag, even a wooden hand mirror. Each item came gift-wrapped in shiny boxes with silk ribbons from her favorite stores. My mother had taken early retirement and was flush with cash. I called her to thank her, after each surprise present. She was reliving my childhood exclamations, when I saw what Santa had brought on Christmas mornings.

During one call, she asked, "Would you come with me to Burnsville, North Carolina? I want to see where I spent my childhood. Visit the old places. It would mean a lot, if you could come along."

"How long?" I delayed my answer.

"What about five days? Could you manage that?" she asked. "You could take the train to D.C., and then we could drive from here. We could go next month, when the leaves will be colorful."

I paused, hesitating. Five days in a car with my mother! I wasn't sure we could be civil for that long. But she was my mother, and she had faced some harsh demons in Burnsville, the place where she was banished to after her father was killed in a car accident. I had to face my demons, my temper, and my feelings of not being good enough when I spent any extended time with my mother. "OK," I told her. "I'll go."

* * *

Sarah and I had edited a twenty-minute video demo of *We're Not in Kansas Anymore*, and had shown it to funders. We were counting on the Rockefeller Foundation, which had already funded us, to give us the post-production money. They wanted us to cut out the footage of Harold's interview about how wonderful the Soviets were to him, before they would give us more funds. Wealthy leftists, part of a Soviet-American grassroots activist group, asked us to cut out the clown scene and Clare's interview about how bad the Soviets were, to secure their donation. The Jewish funders didn't like Stephen's passive attitude about the Holocaust. Our CBS producer turned down broadcasting the story because positive stories about the Soviet Union were not newsworthy at that time. We thought the story was more mixed, but CBS's agenda was covering President Reagan's escalation of Cold War policies.

Sarah and I argued against these changes—it was important to show contradictions, the truth, the grey, not just a black and white point of view. But the funders gave us no more money for the documentary post-production. I applied for various grants but was not hopeful about getting any more funding without censoring our ideas. Patricia had broken up with her millionaire boyfriend, too, so there were no more individual contributions.

Sarah's complaints, her arguments, irritated me, and I exploded, shouted, stomped through the loft. I was a ball wound so tight that it didn't take much for me to scream, cry, and go into overwhelm mode. Sarah and I were tolerating each other to be able to work together. The personal front was tense, full of frustrations.

The season was changing. Fall brought cold nights in the loft, too early for plastic on the windows. I climbed into a steamy hot bath on a Saturday night before the hurricane. Sitting in the tub, my legs stretched out, I felt a deep rumbling in my guts. A completely foreign being inside me uncurled, opened its mouth, and let out a cry, a primordial scream, as if the thing knew the pain of being human, of failure, of the unknown. This being was otherworldly, an alien shouting a message I couldn't understand. It was a growl, a release. Minutes felt like hours. Then, this invader left me as suddenly as it had grabbed me. I was free of its bond. This unconscious reptile held me captive no longer.

My fragile mask fell and shattered. I was raw, no pretenses. I realized that my labels—war correspondent, filmmaker, girlfriend, fiancé, lesbian, bisexual, fatso—were meaningless. They were not me. Before this crisis haunted me; I had felt hopeless, worthless, and lonely. A big shift happened after the creature, the bad juju, destroyed itself by coming out. Who I was did not depend on what I did or what I had or how I looked. The moan I exhaled in the bathtub, soaking in hot water, had no power over me. I could no longer hate myself for being fat, for making a mistake, for my failures, for who I am.

* * *

Sarah stayed up all night watching the arrows point to a red bull's eye labeled N.Y.C. Hurricane Gloria, a force of nature, was going to attack in an hour. I was due at work at 11 o'clock in the morning to waitress at Rozinante. The winds were strong. Then there was a lull. Fed up with the TV news fortune-telling, I stepped outside. Nobody was on the streets. I walked into the eye of the storm, to the restaurant a few blocks away. The owner was there and greeted me. She was surprised that I came to work. There were no customers. The wind started again, blowing hard, pushing the restaurant's large glass windows with its dutifully taped Xs. Nothing really bad happened that day.

I was never the same after that day. I went forward into the world less concerned with outer appearances, discovering what I could do with the resources I had, and wanting to find inner peace within myself.

CHAPTER 9
THE GUIDING SPIRIT

On the first night of our trip, my mother and I stayed deep in the Blue Ridge Mountains, at the Woodfield Inn. The place had the distinct moldy smell of a used bookstore, and there was even a mama black cat with her litter sleeping on the porch to add to the bookstore feel. The inn was the last place of comfort before we headed to North Carolina and its national park wilderness. In the morning, I sat on the 200-year-old porch looking over the surrounding Southern garden, laced with purple gardenia bushes and roses climbing the white gazebo and the tennis court. I rocked on the porch and read Ouspensky's In Search of the Miraculous, about Mr. Gurdjieff's teachings. It spoke of another reality that could exist, a method for living a meaningful life and finding the Divine.

Before this trip, I had stopped at Weiser Bookshop on Broadway, the best-known occult bookstore in the U.S., looking for books to take on this trip. I wanted to know more about Sufism—our Tbilisi guide's dervish stories and Massoud's Al-Ghazali scriptures had made me curious. The old shopkeeper shuffled over to a dusty bookshelf and pointed me to poetry by Rumi and Hafiz, books about the dervishes, and volume after volume on this mystery man, Gurdjieff.

I was intrigued. We shared the same birthday, November 28th. Here was a mystic who had grown up in Alexandropol, Armenia in the late 1800s, been exiled to France after the communists took over in 1917, and had emerged as the darling of the New York spiritual scene from the 20s till the end of his life, though he had died in Paris, in 1949.

In *Views from the Real World*, a collection of Gurdjieff's teachings published posthumously by his followers, I found an obvious, yet startling insight: We have two lives, an inner and outer life. I wanted to know how to navigate both. We needed to consider everything that happened to us by how we felt, both internally and externally. We could change our external attitudes by becoming aware of our internal states, by ceasing to be reactive to outside circumstances, and by changing our internal experiences.

According to Gurdjieff, we would be free if we managed both our interior and exterior aspects of ourselves, but he warned that this was very difficult to achieve.

My mother came out on the porch carrying her overnight bag and motioned for me to get in the car. I was ready; my bag already loaded in the trunk of her brand new forest green TR7 car. The car was a gift she gave herself when she took early retirement. We headed for Burnsville, a small Southern town and my mother's childhood stomping grounds. It was late October, and the leaves had changed colors, but it still felt warm enough to wear shorts. I opted for long corduroys, too self-conscious to show my thick thighs. I didn't define myself by my weight anymore, but I sure didn't want to draw attention to my fat legs. My mother wore linen Bermuda shorts.

"Missy, how about staying at the hotel in Asheville? We can spend two nights there. Let's get the check-in out of the way, first. I think the Biltmore Estate is nearby. We can stop and see it, then go have lunch in Burnsville," my mother plotted, as we drove through the Blue Ridge National Park.

"You mean Vanderbilt's mansion? It says in the guide book that it's the largest privately owned home in the U.S., 178,926 square feet and an example of the gilded age," I said. "Sounds like fun. Yes, let's do it all before lunch."

We pulled into the long gravel driveway. The chateau-styled monstrosity stood centered at the end of a jàrdin a la française.

"Can you get the tickets for the parking and tour?" said my mother, as she handed me her American Express card, and I got out. She drove to the first available parking space, hopped out, and slammed the car door.

When I returned with the tickets, I found her pacing around her car. "Look what I've done—locked the keys in the car," she said.

"The motor's running," I said.

I felt my emotions rise, a knee jerk, exterior attitude reflecting the smirk I felt inside. But I had just read that I could stop this automatic reaction. I took a pause. I breathed.

"This ruins everything, doesn't it?" my mother said.

"Oh, no, not at all. We'll call AAA, and they'll unlock the car for us. It's just a minor delay," I said, starting to change a lifelong habit. My attitude shifted when I observed myself, caught myself, and opened to the moment before reacting.

My mother could be so hard on herself, harder than anyone else was on her. She appreciated the easy solution. I ran back to the ticket office to call for help. The tow truck arrived in fifteen minutes, and in 30 seconds, the mechanic unlocked the door and turned off the car motor. My mother handed him a ten dollar bill. He gave her the car keys.

We walked through the Biltmore's front door and visited the excessively gaudy rooms that were intended to replicate English nobility—samurai armor at the entrance, leading to rooms clothed in red silk wallpaper, decked out in canary yellow armchairs, with heavy carved oak furniture.

"Poor taste," my mother said.

"Nouveau riche at their worst," I said, and we laughed at the shared joke.

In the back of the building, we stumbled upon English gardens, adorned with yellow and red mums in full bloom. They were spread out in geometrical shapes—triangles, rectangles, and trapezoids. Gorgeous. Satisfied with the walk in the gardens, we climbed into the sports car and sped to Burnsville.

On the winding road, as I sat next to my mother while she drove, a flash of a memory came to me from when I was eleven years old. My mother had picked my siblings and me up after school at the end of her workday. I sat in the front and my siblings were in the back seat. She took us to visit our father at George Washington Hospital, after the fire in the kitchen. The panic we felt was palpable and penetrated our senses.

"Your dad is going to die," my mother said in a flat tone, through pursed lips. "This is your last chance to see him."

The doctors gave us reason to believe her. We were told that nobody could survive second and third degree burns over 40 percent of his body. Elena, Wolfgang, and I didn't speak. We were in a self-contained grieving capsule, blasting towards an unknown future. My mother's own father had died in a car accident. She and her mother were both uninjured. They were stranded for hours in the Arizona desert, next to the car crash, until help came. Fathers died, my mother's past had taught her. They left their wives and children behind.

Fortunately, my father didn't die—there was a new medical procedure. My father was the guinea pig, the first test-case to survive the grafting of pig's skin on his body. His chest, back, shoulders, arms, and legs were covered in the animal skin, scarring a good portion of his body, leaving his skin crinkly pinkish. He would later hide it under his strategically chosen clothes. Miraculously, his handsome face was unharmed.

Still, my mother persisted. "Your father nearly died last night. The nurses forgot to give him orange juice," my mother told us, as she drove the tan Buick to the hospital the next day. Her belief that fathers die was hard to shake.

"Mom, when we drove to visit Dad in the hospital you kept telling me he was going to die. You told me 'This is your last chance to see him.' I know the doctors told us he wouldn't survive. But you really insisted," I said, as we got closer to Burnsville. She reviled the town, the horrible hills she had to climb to go to school, her mean grandmother, the loneliness, the absence of her mother who had gone to live in San Francisco.

"Do you think your problem started when you were seven years old? You must have felt so vulnerable, scared, abandoned—maybe this is why you're prone to depression and alcoholism?" I boldly asked.

"Maybe. I hated my father before he died. Then, after he was killed, I dreamed of having a father who would be my savior, could protect me. When I married your father, I believed he would make everything better for me. But that didn't happen. I had to do everything. It was too much. Life was too harsh. I drank and couldn't stop. I'm trying now to be better ..."

"Really, everything is based on the man. But you were ambitious, successful at work, smart. You're a feminist. It can't all be about the man," I said.

"I don't know, for me it's been harder. It was an impossible situation trying to be a mother and wife and work full-time. After the fire, when your father started working again, maybe I would have been better off staying home, raising you kids, like most of my Smith classmates. But, you know, it's never been easy with him."

My parents were a good intellectual match, but mostly, they did not get along. Like my parents, Sarah and I shared similar ideals, but we were drifting apart. I couldn't tell my mother about my love problems, since she didn't know Sarah and I were lovers to begin with. So I listened instead.

"In the deposition for our divorce case, his lordship said how marvelous psychocyclics like himself were because they were up most of the time. He also described how he caused me to lose my credit card by taking a woman from L.A. to Mexico, but he didn't really think I should mind because it hadn't been very expensive, because she was a vegetarian," my mother vented.

"What's a psychocyclic?" I asked.

"You know, someone who is high all the time, like on LSD."

"But mom, those women who raised kids in the suburbs became alcoholics, too. They felt oppressed by that kind of lifestyle, bored even, unfulfilled. When their kids left home, they had nothing to show but an empty house."

"There's no easy answer, Missy. But I'm sure you'll figure something out."

"I want to find a way where I'm not sucked into the trappings of marriage, a job title, or motherhood. I want to live an authentic life, driven from an inner working, not from what society dictates is best."

"What's happened to George?" my mother suddenly asked.

"He left me, went back to Greece. Doesn't really want anything to do with me since I came back from the Soviet Union."

"I'm sorry. He's a good guy. By the way, I was reading this funny book called *Parallel Lives: Five Victorian Marriages* by Phyllis Rose. It's great, complete with a mother's advice to her daughter on her wedding night: 'Lay back and think of England!'"

"You're too much, really," I laughed.

My mother didn't answer, but we both sat in silence, a new kind of silence where we could feel each other and connect in the presence of a true mother-daughter awareness. We could enjoy each other and hold our dreams for each other and ourselves.

Upon arriving in Burnsville, we stopped at the Nu Wray Inn for a traditional Southern-style lunch in the town square. We walked on the stone pathway to the entrance of the colonial guest house and crossed the dark lobby, where a large stone fireplace dominated the seating area. The dining room had long tables covered with white lace tablecloths for family-style seating. The low ceilings, floral wallpaper, and pewter serving dishes were reminiscent of the pre-Civil War period. Next to our table, twelve obese women in bright-colored house dresses passed around fried chicken, ham, macaroni and cheese, coleslaw, and buttermilk biscuits. Blueberry, pecan, cherry, and apple pies were on display on the sideboard. My mother and I joined the locals and piled the food on our plates. My mother didn't mention anything about the calories.

I felt small next to these women, who seemed to weigh over 200 pounds. My mother and I were the thin ones in the room, skinny next to these fat women. There was no one to envy. Body image was a complex issue for me. Everywhere I turned, there were images of skinny, successful women. It was hard not to compare, even when it was with oversized women who were fatter than me. I ate the main course and then the dessert, drank sweet iced tea, experiencing pure delight in non-restraints.

As we walked to the car, I felt overstuffed from all the food I had eaten. We were on our way to visit my mother's grandmother's house, the focal point of a lot of my mother's hurt as a child. Then I began to feel overwhelmed, as I listened to her start to tell the story of how her father died.

"We were on a road trip, me, mom, and dad. It was 1939. Your grandfather was surveying some land, looking for the mineral telluride. He had graduated first in his class at the Colorado School of Mines. Your great uncle, Vernon, my mother's brother, came in second in the same class. That's how they met. We drove for hours through the flattest part of Arizona. I was asleep in the back seat. A drunk driver drove on the wrong side of the road and straight into us. The driver didn't stop, not even to see what happened.

I woke up immediately. I saw my father open the car door and jump out of the car, leaving us behind. All of this happened before the crash. It was like time slowed down. I remembered thinking that my father was trying to save himself and leaving us in the car to die. What happened was he was injured because he jumped out of the car. Mom and I were totally unhurt. If he had stayed in the car with us he would have been safe. He lay on the side of the road, next to our crashed car, bleeding to death. It was hours before a car passed. He died while we watched."

My mother's traumatic memories of the accident, Burnsville, and her grandmother's house all mixed together, a form of acute fear and anxiety, resurfacing anytime she was faced with danger or tough times.

"Missy, I thought I caused my dad's death. God was punishing me because I hated my dad. Dad punished me when he was home."

"Why would your dad do that?"

"Dad was strict and ordered me to do things. I would get mad because mom would ignore me when he was back from his survey trips. I messed things up—sometimes on purpose."

"But why did you think God wanted to punish you?"

"I prayed for my dad to die, and he did," my mother said, with tears in her eyes.

My mother's childhood anger had turned into a curse. The similarities between my mother and Sylvia Plath were tragic. Sylvia wrote in her journal how she hated her father, who died of diabetes complications. Both their fathers had died when they were seven years old. Later that afternoon, we drove past the little house where her grandmother had lived. It looked shabbily perfect, with large pink roses in full bloom on the white gazebo in the backyard. It was not the ugly house Mom had described to me as a child. We hesitated to knock on the door or look inside. It was enough to catch a glimpse from the car window. We drove up the street, past my mother's old grade school next to the Presbyterian Church.

"I hated walking to school. The road was so steep. I had to make this same walk on Sundays. My grandmother held my hand tight, when we walked together to church. I hated Sunday School. Once, I told the Sunday School teacher, 'I'm not going to sing "Jesus Loves Me,"' but she insisted that I stand up and take hold of her hands and sing along. Well, I stood up, and took hold of her hands, but I didn't sing 'Jesus Loves Me.' I sealed my lips tight and disapproval enveloped me, from my heels up to my head. I must have been around ten years old."

The gigantic hill she climbed to school became a gentle slope when we saw it together as adults. My mother also had a good memory of Burnsville, "There was a movie theater in town where I loved to watch Shirley Temple. I think it was called the Yancey Theatre." The negative memories were being replaced by new memories, her past transformed by new circumstances.

During my teenage years, I had no understanding of my mother's pain. To be abandoned by her mother when she needed her most! She needed help to understand that her father's death was not her fault. Her mother had not reassured her. But, now, we were reassuring each other by revisiting these memories.

I felt closer to my mother, now that she shared her childhood in such detail. The stories I had heard as a child had seemed like folklore, but as an adult, I understood they were real experiences, wounds covered by bandages. Wounds that had festered. Now, she was exposing them to light so they could heal.

"Gurdjieff said that we all struggle with negative emotions. They have to reach a critical mass, like locusts swarming, before they can die. Then, these memories can seem more unreal, not so fixed. The air becomes brighter," I told my mother, as we drove out of Burnsville.

"You're so like your father when you talk like this. I was never really interested in this spiritual stuff. I'm more of an atheist at heart."

"You know, he's taken the Bodhisattva vows to attain complete enlightenment?"

"That's a laugh, really. If your father is enlightened, I'm a snail. I don't believe in any of it."

We arrived in Asheville, a Southern town with cute boutiques, coffee shops, and restaurants with verandas. We stopped for mint juleps. No rows, no discontent, no anger. After our drinks and dinner, she took me shopping and bought me a green corduroy pantsuit. I felt and looked great in the new outfit. When I wore the green suit, I knew magic was possible. My mother and I were becoming friends.

We drove out of North Carolina, with a new appreciation for each other, new memories of fun and pleasure, and a few pictures of each other. There was one of me standing next to an old, rusted 1930s truck in a golden field. Another one was of my mother sitting by herself on a stone wall. We were alone together but separate in the photographs. I wished I had put the camera on automatic and taken a picture of us, arms around each other, smiling. Just one picture of the two of us. I would have done it, had I known she would die young. Five years later, at the age of 57, my mother would be gone. I regret that the picture was never taken.

As we left behind the Blue Ridge Mountains, I started to see my mother through fresh, young adult eyes. It was a healing trip for us both.

* * *

At the loft, I was sitting by myself at the kitchen table, drinking a cup of coffee. It was morning before my roommates woke up. I was enjoying spending time apart from Sarah. We still worked together, but we were no longer fully enmeshed in each other's lives.

The rain was streaming down, outside the window. The room was in shadow, except for the light over the table that highlighted the roughness of its wood surface. I tasted the bitter black coffee, awake to the senses of the taste. I was not trying to save calories; I was experimenting with paying attention, changing a habit of enjoying creamy coffee so I could observe myself better. A simple Gurdjieffian exercise.

I was interested in finding a spiritual path that emphasized living out in the world, rather than my father's more monastic, Rinzai Zen warrior tradition. My father was looking more and more like a monk, wearing Japanese heavy cotton temple robes, a wraparound jacket with baggy pants tucked into his boots, and a silver relic pendant around his neck—a strange sight, even in New York City. He had fully immersed himself in the life and philosophies of the East, finding an openness, a reverence for life in the moment. He now had an ability to concentrate that came from his extensive meditation practice. He was less agitated and didn't get irritated as easily. Yet, there was a hardness, a rigidity, and a commitment to a male teacher that I wanted to avoid. The Gurdjieff group had leaders and teachers, but there wasn't the male guru worship that existed in the Zen community in mid-80s.

After the road trip with my mother, I searched for a spiritual teacher. Former neighbors at The Ontario, where I grew up, heard of my quest and gave me the contact information of a Gurdjieff teacher. It was a secret society, and only through word of mouth could you find an authentic group that had descended from Gurdjieff. There were many lookalike groups that named themselves after Gurdjieff, but they were pseudo-spiritual communities, with no firsthand experience of the actual teachings—they were applying ideas from the books, without context or practical experience.

I recognized that all my aims to succeed in life, in film, in work towards changing the world, must come from a shift from within. I had put my efforts into external goals, into action in the world, but my interior world was shaky. The demon I felt in the bathtub during the hurricane was my shadow side. The dark side lived side by side with the light. I wanted to integrate these two sides of me.

Around the time of my birthday and Gurdjieff's birthday, I walked into the Green Cafe on the Upper East Side to meet my new teacher, Sarah. The synchronicity of her sharing a name with my mother and my partner, did not escape me. Past the cash register, I saw her: a woman in her late thirties, blond, dressed in a long skirt and sweater top, seated at a small table for two. I sat down across from her. Her smile exuded a calmness, a deep richness of existence, a knowingness. I immediately felt open with her.

"What do you want from the Work?" Sarah asked me.

"I have been searching all my life for an understanding of life. How to live? Who am I? When I was in Afghanistan I had an experience where I dissolved into Source. I wanted to know more, but I was leery of joining a spiritual group. My father is a Zen Buddhist, which I tried, but I wanted something different, something that didn't require me to go off on retreats, but that I could practice by myself every day. When I was twelve years old, I remember going into a bookstore looking for anything on the meaning of life. I couldn't find much that wasn't Christian. Later, in high school, I read Jane Roberts' channeled Seth Books; Zen and the Art of Motorcycle Maintenance; and Suzuki's Zen Mind, Beginner's Mind. I did the est training, which was developed by Werner Erhard, in my early twenties."

"What draws you to Gurdjieff?" she asked.

"I've been reading Ouspensky's books. Now, I'm reading Gurdjieff's *Beelzebub's Tales to His Grandson*, but I don't understand a word of it."

Sarah smiled.

"Gurdjieff compares us to a house with four rooms. We live in one room, the smallest and poorest, and we don't suspect the existence of any of the other rooms. Then, we learn that there are other rooms, and they are full of treasures. We can seek the keys to these rooms, especially the fourth, which is the most important room. In the fourth room, we become the master of our own house. Gurdjieff taught that only then does the house truly belong to us wholly and forever," she said.

From that day on, we met in this same spot, week after week. I embarked on a journey within, aided by my spiritual guide. A few months after our first meeting, Sarah said, "There's a street person I pass every day. She roams not far from here. I watch this stranger, as she walks down Third Avenue pushing her full shopping cart. This homeless woman rearranges her belongings. Each gesture is precise, majestic, and otherworldly. Things are not what they seem. I see this quality in this person, and I seek the same intention in my life."

"What do you mean?" I asked. I had no idea what she was talking about.

"Continue with the work, and it will all become clear," she said.

In the Gurdjieff tradition, the emphasis was on the practice of the Work, on how to live an ordinary life with exceptional attention, awareness, and observation. Sarah taught me how to meditate, which was called "sitting." Each morning, I closed my eyes, followed the sensations from my head, down my neck, right shoulder, right arm, down to my right foot, and back up. I did the same down and up on my left side.

I practiced the self-observation exercises to learn how to divide my attention. I practiced trying to be aware of my external experiences, while also being aware of my inner state. When I intentionally turned my attention inward and observed myself, I heard a voice that was examining, judging, criticizing all my motives and intentions.

"Why did you raise your voice at your partner when she asked you to make a fundraising call?" said the nagging voice in my head, judging.

Sarah told me not to judge or criticize these observations. Sometimes, I swung in the opposite direction and heard a self-aggrandizing voice.

"You're so brilliant. What an amazing idea. Everyone will love this one."

Sarah told me not to pay any attention to this voice either.

Then, I heard another kind of voice telling me the general rules I imposed on myself. This last voice was the voice of my demons, dictating what I ought to do, what society expected of me. Good girls are not forceful. They don't speak out. They don't make demands. They help others at all costs, compromise, and give to others at the expense of their own desires. I had battled with these voices, and my aim was to not let them inhibit my progress anymore.

Another self-observation exercise that Sarah gave me was to observe myself when walking through a doorway. A whole day would go by and I wouldn't think of the exercise, or I would remember it hours later, while doing something else. Sometimes, I would catch myself in a brief moment as I went through a door. The humbling realization that I was pretty much on automatic most of the day, reactive to outside circumstances, woke me up to how much work I needed to do on myself. My intention to work harder on this interior life kept growing stronger. I intended to free myself, to be more spontaneous, more centered, and more present in the moment.

As I observed myself, I started to ask: "Who is watching me? Who was having all these thoughts of the past and of the future? Who was having these feelings? Then, who forgot and went into automatic mode for hours at a time?"

When I did observe myself, I could only do it in the moment. I had to be present in the moment and observe the now.

At 24 years old, I was practicing sitting daily. The self-observation exercises continued, and now I could feel sensations in my body when I was momentarily awake to the witness within. I became aware of my breath during the day and caught emotions before they erupted. Thoughts were constant, but once in awhile, I could watch them cycling from past to future, judging, worrying, congratulating myself, noticing old values and beliefs that were difficult to bring into the present. I became stronger, went deeper in my meditations.

Time could pass without a barrage of distracting ideas. A calmness would pass through me, unrelated to what I was doing or thinking. I wasn't always running to something, projecting my sense of well-being on achieving a future goal. I could briefly follow my interior moment-to-moment actions. I felt split in a good way, into the part of me that was not aware and was just doing and the part of me that was awake and observing.

My ongoing work over many years with my Gurdjieff teacher Sarah gave me a way to work on emotions that simmered under the surface daily. I was still reacting to Sarah, my partner, who insisted we work 24/7 on all our film projects. There was no personal life except my spiritual life, which she accepted but was not interested in. Sarah was an atheist, like my mother.

The more we worked together, the more platonic our relationship became. I appreciated the new roles Sarah and I created for ourselves as women (beyond cultural roles of mother and lover), but my primary directive was my spiritual pursuit. This desire to evolve to higher forms of integration, consciousness, and connection fundamentally separated us.

When one of our roommates moved out, I rented her room. I had a room of my own, some personal space to be alone in, to contemplate and meditate in every day. My emotions still ran intense, and this room gave me space and time to gain perspective on my life, work, and relationships. During those years my heart still ached for George. I recorded 90-minute cassette tapes about my life in New York and sent them to him. He started to send tapes back filled with his favorite music, Emmylou Harris, Blondie, and Peter Gabriel. We started to create a new partnership, not based on my projected ideals but on maturity, past experiences, and our shared spiritual values. Still, it was a long distance relationship. We were familiar with its limitations and yearnings.

My fiery nature erupted often, and only through observing my emotions would I recognize a buffer and dial down the intensity. My main daily practice was journal writing, meditation, and the Gurdjieff's self-observation exercises. Each morning, I sat, breathed, and observed the sensations in my body. I noticed my breath, watched the emotions surface. For a fraction of a second, I was aware of everything, and then I was lost again. Over and over, I caught a glimmer of myself. A thread was developing, and the effort started to pay off. I could walk the streets with a sense of calmness rooted deep inside me. The emotional eruptions were less frequent and less intense. I was evolving.

My teenage anxiety propelled me out into the world, led me to face many life circumstances: war, peace, love, failure. Yet, there was something else, something I had read for the first time in the book In Search of the Miraculous and other spiritual texts. I felt bliss when I left Afghanistan in that taxi, peaceful when faced with death during my second trip, and one with all and all time during lovemaking with my lovers.

I had a recurrent dream where I was going to this homeless guy for help on our film project. His name was Mr. Pomegranate, and he told me to meet him on the street corner in front of the entrance of a large glass skyscraper. I went there, and he greeted me, all dressed up in a fine Italian suit with a silk tie. He took me up the elevator to his large corner office on the penthouse floor. He sat down at a large glass-topped metal desk, with floor to ceiling windows behind him looking out over the city. He gave me a check, all the funding I needed. I understood that the dream was not about money or about being saved by a man but about acknowledging the resources I had within and giving them to myself.

* * *

As my spiritual practice deepened, my self-confidence poured forth into my self-container, where I could be more my authentic self and less reactive. I embodied Gurdjieff's allegory of the horse, carriage, driver, and master. My father and I had long conversations about our two traditions. We often met at Hatsuhana Sushi Restaurant when he was in New York for business. We would order scrumptious sashimi and drink warmed saki, while we talked about Zen vs. Gurdjieff's teachings.

In the Zen tradition the emphasis was on reaching enlightenment: Just be here now, and connect to Source. The roshi guided the practitioner to higher levels of consciousness during meditations in the sesshins, long extensive retreats; through dokusan, one-on-one private sessions, where a koan was given, a Zen Buddhist riddle like "What is Buddha?"; and dharma transmissions, an intense ritual where the student could be empowered to teach and be the guru, once he or she reached enlightenment.

In Gurdjieff's Work, the emphasis was on the individual practice and self- observation—no real endgame, except to become the Master of one's carriage. In the last chapter of *Beelzebub's Tales*, Gurdjieff wrote about how our body was like the carriage and the horse was the totality of our emotions. The driver, our mind, steered the horse, trying to control our emotions. But this driver could be like a taxi driver, taking any passenger who sat in the back where they wanted to go, changing destinations all the time. So, the true master was the one who knew where she was going and gave the orders to the driver who directed the horse. Most of the time, the horse was unruly, the carriage was broken, and the driver was drunk or half-asleep. The master was often ignorant.

These were spiritual truths that could be found in all traditions. My father and I agreed about the cross-over of the core principles and insights of our understandings of Zen and Gurdjieff.

Three years passed while I practiced with the Gurdjieff Group and, in parallel, Sarah and I worked together on making films. We continued to make films with hospitalized children, which paid the bills, while we carried on fundraising for *We're Not in Kansas Anymore* and *Big Red*. We were no longer lovers. The sexual spark was neutered, but the creative collaboration galloped forward.

For five long years, George and I kept up a long distance relationship via letters, recorded audiotapes, and phone calls. The few times we were able to meet in person, when I visited Greece, we found ourselves more like independent beings than projected, idealized members of the opposite sex. We shared the same interest in spirituality, in becoming better people, and enjoyed a renewed friendship and romance.

In the early spring of 1990, George took a flight from Athens into John F. Kennedy Airport. New York was quiet. A downy white snow covered the streets, muffling the sounds of the city. A friend rented me a room in her penthouse apartment on the Upper West Side. I bought a floral comforter for the twin mattress on the floor and put daisies in a vase on a crate. We both arrived with our suitcases and carried them into the simple room with a window that looked out over treetops and apartment buildings. My spirit soared, I found myself falling in love AGAIN with the same man I had loved for over ten years. We had another chance to explore our relationship and possibly make a commitment to be together.

"What are the chances you would stay?" I asked.

"10%."

Each day I would ask, more in love than the previous day, high in his presence, his tenderness, his voice, his smells.

"20%, 40%, 50%, 80%, 95%," and then the final "100%."

A week later I said, "Let's marry."

Marriage was the only thing on my mind. My certainty was final. There was no doubt left in my heart. I wanted this man. He was the one I wanted to live with. I didn't want to lose him again.

"Your birthday is in two days, April 4th. It would make it easy to remember our anniversary, if we married then," I said.

"OK."

And it was done. George and I went down to city hall and filled out the application for the marriage license. We planned to be back at the city clerk's office 24 hours later for the marriage ceremony. Back at my friend's penthouse apartment, I borrowed the phone. I plugged the push-tone phone into the bedroom's jack in the wall, while sitting on the wood floor, leaning against the mattress and called Sarah.

"I'm getting married tomorrow," I said.

Sarah paused, I could hear her take a deep breath.

"This will make you happy," she said and paused again.

"Can I come?" I felt tears and took a breath, "Yes, I would love that."

"There are no appointments. Let's meet downtown at 3 p.m. at City Hall. Tomorrow," I said.

Then, I called my mother in Arizona, where she had retired at 57 years old. She had always been fond of George, had met him a few times before we had broken up. Mom sounded happy, "Congratulations," she said. "I love you."

"We'll have a real wedding next year, with a white dress and all, when we have time to plan. Maybe we'll have it on the island of Tinos, where George's ancestors came from. But he only has a one-month visa this time, so we need to marry right away so he can stay."

"I understand," she said.

I called my father next. "I'm getting married."

"When?" he asked.

"Tomorrow."

"OK, dear. These moments give us the flash of knowledge, when we take steps that will change our lives forever," my father said. "You have my blessings." He was becoming more and more like a great sage.

I was getting married, really married, the next day. George was completely at ease with the decision, once he agreed, as if he had forgotten his doubts. It was destined, the next scene in a movie already scripted.

The next morning, on my wedding day, I skipped downtown by myself, looking for a dress at my favorite Eileen Fisher on 9th Street, a tiny outlet store where deals were possible. I picked out a blush purple silk dress and a raw beige silk jacket, all for under $100. Around the corner I bought eyeliner, mascara, lipstick, eye shadow, and pantyhose. The city was breezy and tinged with a slight chill in the air. I walked down to Broome Street, up the six flights of stairs, and opened the metal door with the number 6 painted on it, The Lovers' number in the Tarot deck.

Sarah helped me dress, fixed a brown comb in my hair, and loaned me fancy shoes. Then, she presented me with a beautiful bridal bouquet, white and pink roses, tied with a silk ribbon that matched my dress. It was the same lovely color purple.

We took the subway to City Hall. The Brooklyn Bridge behind the stately building reminded me of the yellow brick road to a magical kingdom. We took the elevator to the government waiting room filled with plastic chairs and fluorescent lights.

George was waiting for us in a suit, one he was planning to also use for future job interviews. It was a short line, only a few couples ahead of us. We entered the chamber, facing the American flag on a stand, then had our marriage contract read to us by the Justice of the Peace, a woman who performed this task up to seventy times a day. George's eyes sparkled. He was beaming at me. He had this same look a year later when we married in Tinos, me in a white lace wedding dress and he in a black tux, surrounded by family, friends, and local villagers. The only one missing was my mom.

Sarah and I went to freshen up in the bathroom. There, a huge, spray painted sign greeted us on the stalls, "Another one bites the dust." Sarah took a picture of it. She took more pictures at the ceremony and on the street in front of the Brooklyn Bridge. We were a small troubadour group playing it up for the camera, jumping in the air, clicking our heels. George and I were in love and felt loved. As we descended into the New York subway, my bridal bouquet brought smiles to people's faces. Strangers congratulated us.

My desperate need to feel fulfilled through a sexual relationship was exhausted and released. I joined in this coming together of two people, who loved each other and would share a life together for more than twenty years.

I did not have a fairy tale wedding like Snow White, who married the prince who woke her up. I discovered my prince inside of me. Inside myself, I found the powerful male energies and I married them with my loving female energies. My marriage was a marriage founded on two fully formed individuals who would not be stuck in gender roles.

The power of a relationship is to live life completely, to take responsibility for love, for both pain and joy, and to mature in a mystical, creative way so that both people in the marriage are whole and passionate.

* * *

Seven months after George and I married, twelve days before my birthday, the Tucson sheriff called from Arizona. I stood holding the receiver in my right hand in our bedroom at the Penington Friends House. I recall looking at the lovely cherrywood-framed mirror that hung over the marble fireplace.

"Are you Melissa Burch?" the sheriff asked.

"Yes."

"Are you Sarah Burch's daughter?"

"Yes, I am." I started to tremble.

"Your mother passed last night. Her body is in the city morgue. I'm so sorry for your loss," the sheriff added.

Every cell vibrated with pain inside me. My breath stopped, then I gasped hard, my heart beating fast, sweat drenching the back of my neck. The wave of external circumstances hit me hard.

"Mom died," I told George, who had not taken his eyes off me since I picked up the phone.

My mother wasn't sick. I had seen her a few months back and talked to her regularly on the phone, but she continued to drink heavily. On one phone call, she told me her doctor said she could die any day. The doctor had said that her liver was destroyed, but she laughed at the prognosis when I questioned her. I thought she was joking. She wasn't.

I made arrangements to fly out to her rental home in the desert. George and Sarah accompanied me, while I traveled zombie-like from New York City to Tucson. My father, Elena, and Wolfgang met us at the airport. My father arrived before any of us and checked into a local hotel, room 105, the same as our old apartment number at The Ontario—the last place where Mom, Dad, Elena, Wolfgang, and me all lived together as a family. We took two rented cars to my mother's home.

Outside her house, in the front yard, a saguaro cactus stood like a scarecrow next to my mother's new white Toyota. She had traded in her sports car and bought a more practical car. Inside, we found an African grey parrot and a six- month-old black-brown Briard puppy. Both pets needed attention, but the house seemed in order. A neighbor had cared for the pets for the 48 hours it took for us to arrive. He was the one who had found her lying dead on the floor. Then, I saw this pink-yellow trail running from her bedroom's white wall-to-wall shag carpet to the outside of the bathroom. It wasn't blood but a weird-colored vomit. The sheriff had told me on the phone that she had died in the bathroom.

George and I were lying on Mom's queen size bed, filling the empty space. I cried all night, missing her, remembering her voice, her sayings, and her obsessions with deductive and inductive logic. George stayed up with me, crying, too, at times. My sister, brother, and Sarah slept in the guest bedrooms.

In the morning, I opened her walk-in closet, switched on the light, and chose a purple linen suit for her to wear. I saw her girdles neatly folded on the shelf—she wouldn't need them anymore. I also picked one of my mother's black designer skirts with ruffles at the bottom and a fitted top to wear for the viewing at the funeral parlor.

On the dining room table, the same one we grew up with at The Ontario, was a pile of unopened bills, bank statements, and correspondence. My siblings and I opened the envelopes, which revealed debt—bank accounts overdrawn, her American Express card maxed out, her savings depleted. She had no money, other than her monthly social security and pension checks. Wolfgang opened an envelope, and a $1 bill dropped out.

"Mom has a dollar," he said, "and she's the economist of the family."

We laughed, dissolving some of the tension of discovering the truth. My mother's generosity came at a price. She was utterly broke.

I walked over to her office and sat at her desk, where her Toshiba laptop was opened. The computer was still on. I hit the keyboard, and my mother's film script about Sylvia Plath appeared. It was the last project she worked on. Regrettably, the script has been lost during these past decades.

In Tucson's vacation weather, under sunny blue skies, we were a small tribe gathered for my mother's passing. Thanksgiving was in four days, my birthday in six. I would be twenty-nine years old.

At the funeral parlor, large vases of bright orange and yellow flowers were placed on tables on either side of the viewing room entrance. My mother's body was in the next room, lying in a borrowed mahogany coffin, silk lined, and with large brass knobs. My mother was in the purple suit I had picked out earlier in the morning.

Her limbs were bloated, her face nearly unrecognizable. The makeup drawn on her looked as if a five year old had colored it in a coloring book, red where there should be lips, blue where there should be eyelids, blush where there should be cheeks. I don't remember ever seeing my mother wear pink circles on her cheeks. The color of her skin, a purple undertone, was a dead person's complexion. I could not look at her for long.

I turned and walked out of the room. I looked at the yellow and orange flowers, which smelled of decay, putrid and sickly. My mother was not the body in the other room, a final reminder that our spirit, our love, was not material, did not exist in the physical realm.

The day after the viewing, Elena, Wolfgang, and I picked up our mother's ashes from the funeral parlor in a cardboard box. We drove to the local canyon, to an amusement park ride on a long open train. For five dollars, we could travel through the Sabino Canyon, where many John Wayne films and other Western movies were shot. We brought champagne, plastic cups, and a camera to record the moment when we scattered our mother's ashes. I remembered that her father had also died here.

The park was not busy in the late afternoon. We had timed the trip for the sunset. We climbed on the plastic bench seats and, like kids, we hung our arms and legs out of the train car. We fanned out, each taking a whole bench. The train climbed the mountain, switchbacking at times, other times driving up a 40 degree angle. A rabbit jumped out of the golden brush; I pointed. Elena saw a rattlesnake coiled next to a saguaro cactus. Wolfgang looked up, and we followed his line of vision to an eagle above us. A Gila monster next. A coyote, a raven, a chipmunk, a red fox, an elk. The animals of the canyon popped out of the brush like the Disney version of *Snow White and the Seven Dwarfs*, honoring our mother's passing. Death felt surreal when I was faced with it in Afghanistan but, here, with my mother gone, death was tangible and real.

We reached the summit and dismounted, the only people at the top of the canyon. We would catch the last train down after sunset. The sun was sinking fast, purples, pinks, reds splashed across the horizon. The red earth was jagged and immense. Wolfgang opened the champagne and poured it into plastic cups. We toasted our mother, Mom, who gave us life, who did the best she could, and who brought us here together. We had no regrets.

The rough dust, with small pieces of dried bone, dispersed into the Arizona wind.

When my sister, brother, and I returned to my mother's home in the desert, my father, George, and Sarah came together with us in love and grief. My father told a story about ancient footprints found in volcanic ash and mud.

"A family walked across Africa over a hundred thousand years ago. They each had a heart and a brain. When someone died, they felt the loss as much as we do," he said. "They were no different from us standing here."

My father then told a Zen story about searching and eventually finding hoof prints on a riverbank:

> *The presence of the Ox is sensed, and the journey begins.*
> *When the hoof prints are found, the teachings of the path*
> *are found. Then, we glimpse the Ox, something beyond*
> *our common personalities, and we catch it. We tame the*
> *Ox, become a friend with our inner selves. An inner*
> *stillness exists, when we leave the Ox behind. We find*
> *the Absolute Truth, emptiness, wholeness, and beingness.*
> *Now, we return to living in the world as a realized being.*

The Ox, a metaphor for enlightenment, left hoof prints on a riverbank. In the Zen story, these hoof prints meant the discovery of the path beyond ecstatic experiences, accepting death, the flow, facing the shadow; there was the alchemy of life and the spiritual path.

When I returned home, I walked the streets of Manhattan. I trained to follow my breath and the emotions that now pulsated with waves of sadness. I now had a spiritual muscle to deal with intense emotions. The shock of my mother's death woke me up to face death, mortality, grief, and helped me to integrate the good and the bad mother in me.

These messages spontaneously came from the unconscious. The awakening from within arose from an understanding of myself. The male and female energies pointed out a direction to recognize the nature of the mind and find the path. From taking risks, being courageous, and discovering the unknown—the hidden, the shadow—I discovered the life I needed to lead.

EPILOGUE
FINDING MY VOICE

"To find out what is truly individual in ourselves, profound
reflection is needed; and suddenly we realize how profoundly
difficult the discovery of individuality in fact is."

~ C.G. Jung

My forays into war, into male territory, followed by a full swing
into female groups, were ways of running away from a difficult mother. Yet they tore openings in my psyche. A spiritual quest
began. Meaningful messages sparked a new clarity in me. My actions
were no longer reactions to deep-seated emotional issues but chances
to become free and conscious.

With this new energy, a shift in perception and commitment
to fully expressing myself led to a new venture that began during
the late 80s. Sarah and I gathered a group of friends, some from the
earlier Women in Limbo group, and together we crammed into the
Knot Room, a red, cocoon-like back space at the Knitting Factory on
Houston Street. Occupying the well-worn, red velvet theater seats,
this modest group of women faced the stage, where each woman
took a turn standing and telling her story. And that is how Sarah
and I brought to life the second Women in Limbo, a reincarnation of
the Limbo Lounge from over five years before. Drawing inspiration

from our partnership in filmmaking, as well as from theater, photography, art, and autobiographical methods, we devised a specific format for the group. This time, we were a feminist, grassroots artist group, with a strict performance art format:

> *Women, bring your poems, your personal stories, your songs, your voice. Tell us what you really think. Bring your slides of your family, your art, your life, your objects. Scratch those slides, make words, draw cartoons. Get on a stage and perform. All men and women are invited to watch.*

Our women artist collective would produce multi-media art on a weekly theme. There would be no more funders, gatekeepers, producers, or academics rejecting our work and stopping us. We would just do it!

Week after week, five to eight New York women, mostly artists of different ages, primarily 20- to 40-year-olds of different ethnic and economic backgrounds—lovers, lesbians, bisexuals, grandmothers, mothers, and daughters—created eight- to ten-minute, autobiographical one-woman shows on a given topic. We bore witness and cheered each other on subjects as diverse as sexuality, work, body image, creativity, war, and peace. We expounded our message from our hearts and souls in solidarity.

The new Women in Limbo was raw, underground, and passionate. We no longer hosted the usual feminist formats of panels, circles, and speakers. Instead, we took our darkest secrets and brought them to light. We felt "limbo" was empowering because it was not part of the establishment, and the Catholic spiritual meaning of the concept of "limbo," caught between heaven and hell, made us hard to define and mysterious. We proudly wore our black T-shirts printed with "Women in Limbo" in white letters.

We believed in the power of personal stories, as a way to share women's points of view that were not represented in the mainstream media or male- dominated art world. One of our motivations was to protest the U.S. invasion of Iraq and remind people of the evils of war. We were looking for a vehicle to express our outrage and to be heard publicly. At the end of the individual performances, an MC from Women in Limbo would encourage the women in the room to share their personal experiences about the topic. We discouraged questions and answers or experts delivering advice. Week after week, in the back room of the Knitting Factory, we talked, cried, shouted, and sang on Sundays. It was a ritual and our religion of sorts.

When it was my turn to stand on the familiar stage, I looked at my comrades—an audience of twenty people. Most of them I knew well, though there were a few new faces. I gave Sarah my ten slides, a collection of photos, images, and scratched words to project on a white sheet hung on the back brick wall.

I felt like I was inside a safe womb, in this earthy red space. The lights were darkened, casting shadows on the stage. This was an opportunity to tell my story, my truth ...

"Here I am, 21. I smoked hashish on my birthday in Pakistan, waiting for Commander Doc to take me across the border into Afghanistan. No, I'm not a pothead."

The audience laughed at the tough girl photo of me holding a Kalashnikov in Kandahar.

"There was a magnetic force drawing me to adventure and reporting the news ..."

The slide of *The New York Times'* article about Istalif, Commander Massoud, and the Panjshir Valley projected behind me.

"The first trip to Afghanistan worked some kind of magic on me. I developed strength in the face of danger, relied on intuition that saved my life, and had an ecstatic experience. All of this made me a new person—less anxious, more free in myself, and able to handle what would come next."

I turned around to face the back wall and clicked the remote. The next slide came up showing my mother smiling at me from The Ontario's porch. Tears welled up inside me.

"My mother, our mothers, what influence they have over us ... even when they've died. My mother was an alcoholic, but she was so much more. She wanted more from life than just being a mother and a wife. But she struggled to find a way. I'm still trying to figure it out ..."

I paused.

"I had to reach rock bottom, a breaking point and, when I reached it, I felt peaceful and calm."

Click. The words "Women in Limbo," scratched on a black slide. Blue, yellow, and white light letters shone behind me.

"Now, I'm 31, and I want to produce a television series. Here. Now. Where our voices count. Where the feminine matters, and the creative power is expressed in all our complexities. We're political. Women in Limbo is political. This IS consciousness raising!"

Click. A slide of Red Square; the teenagers from Visions of Peace grinned at the camera.

"History happens outside of us, but we're a part of its matrix. The last Soviet soldier left Afghanistan in 1989. I protested, with many of you, the Gulf War in Iraq in 1990. In 1991, we watched on TV as Gorbachev resigned and the Soviet Union dissolved. We stared at the news footage of tanks rolling into Moscow's Red Square, the old babushka women standing firm in front of them, the Lenin statues destroyed and toppled over, the Communist Party crumbling … The glories of the Soviet Union after World War II were over."

Click. The puppets, Sarah and Alexi the naval officer, shaking hands.

"The era of *Big Red* was over, too. I want to honor with bittersweet recognition that, in some way, Sarah and I participated in the unfolding of history. Americans are no longer fearful of the Big Red Soviet Communists."

Click. A photo of the Wind River Range mountains in Wyoming that I took when I was a teenager, where I first discovered that pushing beyond my comfort zone could transform me.

"The creative vision asks me to look at the depths of myself, to stand present in the whirlwind of life, and to face everything and avoid nothing. I transform things outside of me by transforming myself.

"Transformation cannot only be personal. It has to include our community, our nation, our world, all sentient beings, the cosmos. I believe in the evolutionary future, what has not existed before. I believe that existence is fundamentally good, beautiful, and true, but it takes high levels of attention, intention, and conscious action in the Now."

Click. "I AM" scratched on a black slide. Golden light letters shone on the lit sheet.

"I am the eternal Being and evolutionary Becoming. I want to stay open, penetrate my true nature, and connect to something much grander than me—the infinite, the Divine, the creative impulse. I'm on a spiritual path. There's no gender on the path, but I am a New Woman. I have a conscious awareness of wholeness merging with the Divine feminine creative impulse."

Click. Clouds drawn on the black slide.

"I had a dream that I had found a three-part solution for life. The first solution comes when you go out in life. Face your fears and do it anyway, be courageous—Grace will offer you a peak spiritual experience or an Aha moment that changes your life or clear directions for the next steps. The second solution happens when you follow your intuition and move into the flow of life. And, finally, the third solution, the hardest really, appears when you face your demons, bring light into your shadows, free yourself to connect to the Divine 100%."

Click. The tenth image, blown up behind me, of the Zen Ox herding pictures, which culminated in the hero, perfectly at peace, walking unnoticed through the village streets.

"My journey took me through war and peace, searching to integrate the male and female aspects of myself, so I could fulfill my individual human destiny. I know a life well-lived is a life lived from the inside out, directed from an inner knowing, full of mistakes, hard times, and joy."

When the staged performances were broadcast on PBS, I watched myself as a young woman facing my demons, my past, my pain, reconciling opposites—light emerged from darkness. I felt like an alchemist who reconciled with my mother, found a spiritual path, and healed my relationships. I channeled my urges through creative uniqueness. The Creator in me became conscious of my creation, and the woman became conscious of herself. I woke up.

ACKNOWLEDGEMENTS

It takes a village to sustain a debut memoirist. My ability to jump in the deep end of any endeavor is only possible because of my husband, family, and friends who come to cheer me each step of the way. Thank you, George, for encouraging me to tell our story as honestly as I could. I am grateful to my siblings and father who supported me to share our family stories. I love you all.

Susana started me on this path when we woke each other up at 6 a.m. to write. My editors, Julie Gallagher, Alexandria Marzano-Lesnevich, and Ellen Daly, were my first critics, taught me how to be a better writer, and guided me to find my voice. My final editor, Arlinda Shtuni, knew what questions to ask to bring out great ideas and shape a book that is the best it could be.

Susan Dowds, Julie Matthaei, Sue Halliday, and David Yeager cleaned up the grammatical errors and typos. Dawn Jordan kept the momentum going by sharing all her good vibrations. Jean LeVaux inspires me by her wisdom. Leslie Sederlund provides so much grace to all who love her. Kate Soudant is my go-to person for all my crazy ideas; she read my shitty first draft and wanted to read more. Elena has the biggest heart and knows just what to say when life gets hard. Cornerstone Village Cohousing was my home and sanctuary, while I retreated into a writer's life. I am more than grateful to all my writer colleagues, editors, friends, and co-housers for their help.

GrubStreet was my school of choice and gave me a place to grow as a writer. Turkey Land Cove Foundation gave me my first writing residency. When Words Count was my gourmet writing residency in Vermont. Martha Bullen, Mark Malatesta, Miriam Hawley, Maxim Uncu, John Willig, and Linda Sivertsen and Danielle LaPorte's the Beautiful Writer's Group have been great at shaping everything from query letters to improving my website and advising on marketing and contracts.

My literary agent, Susan Schulman, told me she loved my book, which made me feel like I crossed the threshold from writer to soon-to-be-published author. Howard Aster at Mosaic Press is the midwife for my memoir to get out in the bookstores. Matthew Goody is shepherding the book through all the publishing stages. Thank you, Susan, Howard, and Matthew, for your professional support.

My heart goes out to the people of Afghanistan, and I wish for peace and well-being to all. My friends at Women in Limbo, you know who you are, were the best women's artist group anyone could ask for. My lovers, please know that I will always love you and care about you.

These stories are for you, Alex, so you can know that your mother was more than a mother. I love you more than you could ever imagine.

~ Melissa

ABOUT THE AUTHOR

Melissa Burch has worked as a writer, filmmaker, producer, and former war journalist for the BBC, CBS, and other networks. Her team was one of the first documentary crews in the Soviet Union at the height of the Cold War, and a story about her in Afghanistan was featured in *The New York Times*.

Burch was the executive producer of "Women in Limbo Presents," a national public television series about women's lives, and she served as President of the New York Film/Video Council. Her book, *The Four Methods of Journal Writing: Finding Yourself Through Memoir*, was a #1 Amazon bestseller and is still in the top 10 in its category. Also a homeopath, she co-founded the Catalyst School of Homeopathy, and produced and hosted one of the first successful radio shows on Voice America on homeopathy. When she's not cooking dinner for friends and family, she enjoys traveling and her spiritual practice.

My Journey Through War and Peace is the first memoir of Burch's Pathfinder Trilogy.

DISCOVER MORE ABOUT *MY JOURNEY THROUGH WAR AND PEACE*

Receive behind-the-scenes photos, films and more stories from Afghanistan, the Soviet Union, and Soho in New York City when you go to www.melissa-burch.com/reader and enter the code: READER.

Visit the author's website, www.melissa-burch.com, for more information on upcoming events, podcasts and ways to enter the conversation on spirituality, adventure, and feminine journeys.